The Pocket Rumi Reader

The Pocket
Rumi Reader

Edited by
Kabir Helminski

SHAMBHALA
Boston & London
2001

Shambhala Publications, Inc.
Horticultural Hall
300 Massachusetts Avenue
Boston, Massachusetts 02115
www.shambhala.com

12 11 10 9 8 7 6 5

Printed in Canada

♾ This edition is printed on acid-free paper that meets the American
National Standards Institute z39.48 Standard. Distributed in the
United States by Random House, Inc., and in Canada by Random
House of Canada Ltd

Cover art by Ingrid Schaar.

Library of Congress Cataloging-in-Publication Data
Jalal al-Din Rumi, Maulana, 1207–1273.
[Selections. English. 2000]
The pocket Rumi reader / edited by Kabir Helminski.
p. cm. — (Shambhala pocket classics)
ISBN-13 978-1-57062-739-2 (paper)
ISBN-10 1-57062-739-8
1. Sufi poetry, Persian—Translations into English.
I. Helminski, Kabir Edmund, 1947– II. Title. III. Series.
PK6480.E5 H4513 2000
891'.5511—dc21   00-041993

The Logos is digging a channel
for water to reach the next generation.
During every generation
there is one who brings the word of God;
still the sayings of those
who have come before are helpful.

MATHNAWI III, 2537–2538

Contents

Introduction
Our Master Jalâluddin

WHO IS THIS RUMI who has become one of the most popular voices on the contemporary literary and spiritual scene? Why does he speak so compellingly to our sensibilities at this time? What need does he fill? What wound does he help to heal? How is it that a thirteenth–century Islamic saint should become the darling of so many who profess an interest in neither poetry nor spiritual discipline? In the mosques, in academia, in the cafés, and in the studios of Hollywood people are reading and, moreover, *quoting* Rumi.

There is no doubt that he is one of the great literary figures of all time. Within Islamic cultures, especially from the Balkans, through Turkey, Iran, to Pakistan and India, he is deeply loved. His works include a massive collection of lyric poems (*ghazels* and *rubaiyat*) as well as the six-volume *Mathnawi*, a collection of rhymed couplets that weaves together a rich fabric of stories, humor, and spiritual teaching.

The pivotal event in Rumi's life was his meeting with an enigmatic, peripatetic saint named Shamsi Tabrizi. Their encounter somehow kindled a creative and spiritual fire in Rumi that burned for the rest of his life. Rumi saw a reflection of the Divine in Shams; through this relationship, Rumi experienced the Divine with an unprecedented power. In some of Rumi's more ecstatic verses the boundaries between the Divine and the human are blurred. Yet Sufis have always maintained a fastidious distinction between the servant (the human being) and Lord (the Divine). In the mysticism of Islam there is no room for idolatry, material or human.

It is a poetic tradition, especially in the odes and quatrains, to push the metaphors of sensual love and intoxication to their limits, for nothing else can convey the overwhelming nature of the encounter with the Divine. In our Western literary tradition we have not been prepared for this union of the sensual and the spiritual. Our own cultural history has bifurcated: religion in one direction and literature in another. The division was much less pronounced within Islam—in fact, it was practically nonexistent. The Sufis, especially, were neither puritanical nor sensually indulgent. They followed the middle way of Muhammad, which included marriage, a socially useful livelihood, and a life "in the world but not of it."

In Rumi we have a model of the potential harmony between the physical and the spiritual, the heart and the mind, the finite and the Infinite, the human and the Divine. Rumi was not a narrowly "religious" personality, nor was he a proponent of some form of mystical eroticism, nor was he a Promethean rebel. It would surprise many that this passionate and ecstatic man of God made a living during his entire life partly through legal consultations within the framework of Islamic law. He prayed and fasted as any Muslim would, but he challenged the hypocritical and one-dimensional "religion" that is always the enemy of real spirituality.

Mevlâna Jalâluddin Rumi penetrated to the heart of Reality and returned with the fragrance and flavor of Truth. Not only is he one of the greatest literary geniuses, but, perhaps more importantly, he also addresses the most important subject that can be addressed: the human being's relationship with the Divine, with Truth itself. While entertaining, inspiring, informing, and subtly guiding us, Rumi's words touch us at the level where we most need to be touched: the very depths of our hearts.

In doing so, Rumi never places himself in an exalted position in relation to his readers. He is a human being like us, though perhaps more patient, more humble, more forgiving, more flexible than most. This is another aspect of his greatness: that there was no discrepancy between his words and his life.

His humanness and his approachability, however, may mislead us if it causes us to reduce his thought to our own level. Yet we can only begin where we are, and everyone takes from Mevlâna what she or he can. Our culture, I am sure, is only beginning to understand what is contained in Rumi, and the challenge we face is to be able to map his insight and wisdom to our own human experience.

Kabir Helminski

Postscript: Much of this material has been published before, although the quatrains are new, as well as "The Tale of the Bedouin and His Wife." Many of the poems that had no titles have been given titles, and I have revised about fifteen percent of the previously published material.

The Pocket Rumi Reader

1

RUBAIYAT

*Kabir and Camille Helminski
with Lida Saedian*

33

In comfort and abundance the Friend raised
    me.
With vein and skin He tailored this ragged
    body.
It's just a robe worn by a Sufi, the heart.
The whole universe is a *khaneqah**and He is
    my Shaikh.

36

When I am with you our loving
won't let me sleep.
Away from you the tears won't let me sleep.
God, it's amazing to be awake both nights,
But how different these awakenings are!

---

*Sufi training center.

42

I have no companion but Love,
no beginning, no end, no dawn.
The Soul calls from within me:
"You, ignorant of the way of Love,
set Me free."

51

I dreamed of the most exquisite Cupbearer,
a glass of red elixir in hand,
perfect in servanthood.
Could this be our real master?

55

The lover is forever like a drunkard
whose secrets spill out,
forever mad, frenzied, and in love.
To be self-conscious is to worry about
    everything,
but once drunk, what will be will be.

57

Love is the path and direction of our Prophet.
We are born from Love; Love is our mother.
O Mother, hidden behind the body's veil,
concealed by our own cynical nature.

62

If you desire the self, get out of the self.
Leave the shallow stream behind
and flow into the river deep and wide.
Don't be an ox pulling the wheel of the plow,
turn with the stars that wheel above you.

67

At times I would say I had self-control.
At times I felt like a prisoner of myself.
All that's passed. I'm no longer captivated by
    myself.
The lesson I took from this:
not to be taken by myself.

388

I said, My heart wants a kiss from You.
You say: "The price of a kiss is Life."
My heart came up beside me and said:
"It's a cheap down payment."

403

To us a different language has been given,
and a place besides heaven and hell.
Those whose hearts are free
have a different soul,
a pure jewel excavated from a different mine.

491

Whoever sees You and doesn't smile,
whose jaw doesn't drop with awe,
whose qualities fail to increase in a thousand
     ways,
can only be the mortar and bricks of a prison.

494

Someone who received
half a loaf of bread from heaven
and because of her soul's attainment
was given a little nest,
someone who neither desires anybody
nor is desired by anyone—
may she live happily,
for she owns a happy universe.

511

With the Beloved's life-giving waters,
there is no disease.
In the Beloved's garden of Union,
there are no thorns.
They say between our hearts
there's a shutter we can open,
but what is there to open if no walls remain?

549

O pure people who wander the world,
amazed at the idols you see,
what you are searching for out there,
if you look within, you yourself are it.

556

O daylight break, so particles may resound,
so the atmosphere and the heavens will turn,
and so souls, headless and legless, will dance.
Let me whisper into your ear where this all
    goes on.

558

Love, they think You are both angelic
    and human.
They think You are more potent
than the seal of Solomon.
They think You are the life force
within the body of the universe.
But the way I live with You
is not what they think.

561

O tribe, more beautiful than moonlight,
how can you tolerate your muddy existence?
You who have drowned yourself in the tavern,
wake up. It is day. Why are you asleep?

569

The way the Beloved can fit in my heart,
two thousand lives could fit in this body of
    mine.
One kernel could contain a thousand bushels,
and a hundred worlds pass through
the eye of a needle.

666

Whoever gets caught in Your curls,
whether dead or nonexistent, will come
    into life.
You ask of me not to lose myself
in drunkenness, but it's inescapable.
Whoever drinks the wine gets drunk.

670

I am in love with You.
What's the use of giving me advice?
I have already drunk the poison.
What's the use of candy?
They say, "Bind his feet in chains,"
but they can't bind up my crazy heart.

682

Whoever witnessed existence in pure meaning,
and in materiality found nothingness?
Whoever witnessed the Isness of the universe
And within existence recognized nonexistence?

686

The dervish who offers the secrets of the
    universe
gives away a kingdom in every moment.
He doesn't beg for bread;
a dervish bestows life.

674

In love there is no low or high point,
neither consciousness, nor the lack of it.
There is no leader, no shaikh, no follower,
but there are hidden ways, slight of hand, and
    revelry.

667

Whoever has a particle of heart in her breast
will have a hard time living without Your love.
With the curling links of Your locks
anyone one who remains sane is mad.

1078

Have the aspiration of a falcon
and the pride of a leopard.
At the time of the hunt be graceful,
and be victorious at times of war.
Don't get too involved
with the nightingale and the peacock.
One is all words and the other all colors.

1082

I spent some time around people,
but fidelity I neither saw nor smelled in them.
It's better to conceal ourselves
from the eyes of the people,
like water in iron and fire in stone.

1088

The secrets of the truth won't be revealed
through asking too many questions,
nor by giving up all possessions and glories,
but only beyond fifty years,
when your hearts and your eyes are bloody.
From all this talk, no one finds the way to
    ecstasy.

1091

In this world are so many filled with spirit
    like Jesus.
How could it be filled with so many
    false prophets?
How could it be filled with heart-
    darkening brine,
when the water-skin of the universe
is brimming with such pure water?

1092

I have a self that is stubborn, drunken
and won't mind its own business.
I have a beloved who is delicate,
impatient, and easily saddened.
From me to my beloved the prophet is God.
And from the beloved to me
    God is the messenger.

1129

He wishes me to get out of myself.
He wishes me to sit in freedom.
I was constantly involved with ambition,
and now he tells me to break all the chains.

1131

I always see the remedy in pain.
I see the subtle gift and fidelity
in angry quarrels and betrayals.
When I look down, I don't see the earth.
And when I look up,
I don't see the vault of the sky.
Whatever I glance at I see You.

1133

I desire fire from Your burning sorrow,
and I want to take cover
under the dust of Your threshold.
I am in a death struggle with my ailments
and from Your presence, I ask
    a moment of happiness.

1138

I could reach great heights with Your love,
and with longing for You
I will increase a hundredfold.
They ask, "Why are you circling him?"
O ignorance, I am circling myself.

1228

My turban, my robe, and my head—
all three are appraised for less than a dirham.
Have you not heard of my universal fame?
I am nobody, nobody, nobody.

1229

Curse at me. I am drunken with Your curses
and Your pleasing death wishes.
Bring me the poison; I'll drink it like nectar.
I am tamed by you, tamed by you, tamed by you.

1233

Last night my Beloved was giving me pleasure.
I told the night, do not reveal my secrets.
Night said, look around yourself.
You already have the sun; how can I
    bring the dawn?

1238

I am mad, but they repeatedly ask my advice.
I am a stranger, yet they don't banish me.
They are like ignorant *hashishin*,*
who come in the night
and don't recognize me.
But if the day breaks,
they would know who I am.

*People who use hashish while committing a crime.

1241

You left and I cried tears of blood.
My sorrow grows. It's not just that You left.
But when You left my eyes went with You.
Now, how will I cry?

1242

During the day I praised You and I didn't know.
At night I laid with You and I didn't know.
I had suspected that I was myself,
but I was entirely You and I didn't know.

1243

One day drinking wine in Your tavern of ruin,
I offered this robe of mud and water
    for more wine.
Then I saw that the whole world is built
from these ruins of Yours.
Continually being built and I was destroying it.
That's what I was doing.

1246

The moment I first heard of love
I gave up my soul, my heart, and my eyes.
I wondered, could it be that
the lover and the beloved are two?
No, they have always been one.
It is I who have been seeing double.

1247

You were an ascetic
and I turned you into a singer.
You were mute and I turned you into a bard.
Within the universe no one knew
your name nor any sign of you.
I sat you down and made you
a revealer of secrets.

1616

We are puppets in the hands of God.
The power is His; we are all beggars.
Why are we always trying to outdo each other.
when we have all come from the same home?

2

GHAZELS

Kabir Helminski

The Root of the Root of Your Self*

Don't go away, come near.
Don't be faithless, be faithful.
Find the antidote in the venom.
Come to the root of the root of your self.

Molded of clay, yet kneaded
from the substance of certainty,
a guard at the Treasury of Holy Light—
come, return to the root of the root of your self.

Once you get hold of selflessness,
you'll be dragged from your ego
and freed from many traps.
Come, return to the root of the root of your self.

You are born from the children of God's
   creation,
but you have fixed your sight too low.
How can you be happy?
Come, return to the root of the root of your self.

---

*All translations in this chapter are by Kabir Hel-
minski except as noted.

Although you are a talisman protecting
   a treasure,
you are also the mine.
Open your hidden eyes
and come to the root of the root of your self.

You were born from a ray of God's majesty
and have the blessings of a good star.
Why suffer at the hands of things that don't
   exist?
Come, return to the root of the root of your self.

You are a ruby embedded in granite.
How long will you pretend it isn't true?
We can see it in your eyes.
Come to the root of the root of your self.

You came here from the presence of that fine
   Friend,
a little drunk, but gentle, stealing our hearts
with that look so full of fire; so,
come, return to the root of the root of your self.

Our master and host, Shamsi Tabrizi,
has put the eternal cup before you.
Glory be to God, what a rare wine!
So come, return to the root of the root of
    your self.

Love Is a Stranger

Heart came on solid footing with breath refined
to warn the best of communities.
Heart placed your head
like a pen on the page of love.

We are joyous pennants in your just wind.
Master, to where do you dance?

Toward the land of liberation,
toward the plain of nonexistence.

Master, tell us which nonexistence you mean.
The ear of eternity knows the letter of eternity.

Love is a stranger with a strange language,
like an Arab in Persia. I have brought a story;
it is strange, like the one who tells it.
Listen to your servant.

Joseph's face enlightened the well in which
   he hung.
His imprisonment became a palace
with orchards and meadows, a paradise,
a royal hall, and a chamber of sanctity.

Just as you toss a stone into the water,
the water at that very moment parts
    to receive it.
Just as a cloudy night is dispelled by
    a clear dawn,
from his humiliation and loss he views
    high heaven.

Reason, do not envy my mouth.
God witnesses the blessings.
Though the tree drinks from hidden roots,
we see the display of its branches.
Whatever the earth took from heaven,
it yields up honestly in spring.

Whether you have stolen a bead or a jewel,
whether you have raised a flag or a pen,
the night is gone and day has arrived,
and the sleeper shall see what he has dreamed.

The Intellectual

The intellectual is always showing off;
the lover is always getting lost.
The intellectual runs away, afraid of drowning;
the whole business of love is to drown
   in the sea.
Intellectuals plan their repose;
lovers are ashamed to rest.
The lover is always alone,
even surrounded with people;
like water and oil, he remains apart.
The man who goes to the trouble
of giving advice to a lover
gets nothing. He's mocked by passion
Love is like musk. It attracts attention.
Love is a tree, and lovers are its shade.

A New Rule

It is the rule with drunkards to fall upon each
    other,
to quarrel, become violent, and make a scene.
The lover is even worse than a drunkard.
I will tell you what love is: to enter a
    mine of gold.
And what is that gold?

The lover is a king above all kings,
unafraid of death,
not at all interested in a golden crown.
The dervish has a pearl concealed
under his patched cloak.
Why should he go begging door to door?

Last night that moon came along,
drunk, dropping clothes in the street.
"Get up," I told my heart,
"Give the soul a glass of wine.
The moment has come
to join the nightingale in the garden,
to taste sugar with the soul-parrot."

I have fallen, with my heart shattered—
where else but on your path, and I
broke your bowl, drunk, my idol, so drunk,
don't let me be harmed, take my hand.

A new rule, a new law has been born:
break all the glasses and draw near
  to the glassblower.

Didn't I Say?

Didn't I say, "Don't go there; I am your friend.
In this mirage of existence, I am the fountain
    of life."
Even if your anger takes you
a hundred thousand years away,
in the end you will return, for I am your goal.
Didn't I say, "Don't be content with
    earthly forms;
I am the designer of the intimate chamber of
    your contentment."
Didn't I say, "I am the sea, and you are a single
    fish;
don't strand yourself on dry land; I am your
    clear sea."
Didn't I say, "Don't get caught
in the trap like a helpless bird;
I am the power of flight—your feet and your
    wings."
Didn't I say, "They will waylay you and make
    you cold;
I am the fire and your warm desire."
Didn't I say, "They will implant their qualities
    in you

until you forget that the best qualities are here."
Didn't I say, "You do not know from
    what direction
your affairs are put in order."
I am the Creator beyond directions.
If light is in your heart, find your way home.
If you are of God, know your Benefactor.

A House for the Naked

It's late and it's raining, my friends;
let's go home. Let's leave these ruins
we've haunted like owls.
Even though the blind ones beckon us,
let's go home. All the reasons offered
by the sensible, dull, and sorrowful
can't darken our hearts now;
nor can all this phantom love play,
this imaginary paradise hold us back.
Some see the grain but not the harvest.
Don't ask too many "hows" or "whys."
Let beasts graze.
Come home to the real celebration and music.
Shams has built a house for the naked and the
    pure.

Like Sunlight upon the Earth

I am from you, and at the same time,
you have devoured me.
I melt in you since through you I froze.
You squeeze me with your hand,
and then you step on me with your foot.
This is how the grape becomes wine.
You cast us like sunlight upon the earth.
And our light, passing through the body
as if it were an open window to our Source,
returns, purified, to You.
Whoever sees that sun says,
"She is alive,"
and whoever sees only the window says,
"She is dying."
He has veiled our origin in that cup of pain
    and joy.
Within our core we are pure;
all the rest is dregs.
Source of the soul of souls, Shams, the Truth of
    Tabriz,
a hundred hearts are afire for you.

The War Inside

Rest your cheek, for a moment,
on this drunken cheek.
Let me forget the war and cruelty inside myself.
I hold these silver coins in my hand;
give me your wine of golden light.
You have opened the seven doors of heaven;
now lay your hand generously on my tightened
    heart.
All I have to offer is this illusion, my self.
Give it a nickname at least that is real.
Only you can restore what you have broken;
help my broken head.
I'm not asking for some sweet pistachio candy,
but your everlasting love.
Fifty times I've said,
"Heart, stop hunting and step into this net."

Buy Me from My Words

Before now I wanted
to be paid for what I said,
but now I need you
to buy me from my words.
The idols I used to carve
charmed everyone. Now I'm drunk
on Abraham and tired of idols.
An idol with no color or scent
ended my whole career.
Find someone else for the job.
A happy madman without a thought,
I have swept the shop clean.
If something enters my mind,
I say, "Leave. You're a distraction."
Whatever is coarse and heavy, I destroy.
Who should be with Layla?
Someone who can be Majnun.*
The man holding up this waving flag
actually belongs to the other side.

*Layla and Majnun are mythic lovers of Persian lit-
erature. Majnun was "crazy" with his love, and
Layla, though not particularly beautiful to others,
was totally beautiful to Majnun.

This Marriage

May these vows and this marriage be blessed.
May it be sweet milk,
this marriage, like wine and halvah.
May this marriage offer fruit and shade
like the date palm.
May this marriage be full of laughter,
our every day a day in paradise.
May this marriage be a sign of compassion,
a seal of happiness here and hereafter.
May this marriage have a fair face and a good
    name,
an omen as welcome
as the moon in a clear blue sky.
I am out of words to describe
how spirit mingles in this marriage.

Clothes Abandoned on the Shore

Your body is here with us,
but your heart is in the meadow.
You travel with the hunters
though you yourself are what they hunt.

Like a reed flute,
you are encased by your body,
with a restless breathy sound inside.

You are a diver;
your body is just clothing left at the shore.
You are a fish whose way is through water.

In this sea there are many bright veins
and some that are dark.
The heart receives its light
from those bright veins.

If you lift your wing
I can show them to you.
You are hidden like the blood within,
and you are shy if I touch.

Those same veins sing a melancholy tune
in the sweet-stringed lute,
music from a shoreless sea
whose waves roar out of infinity.

The Pull of Love

When Hallaj found union with his beloved,
it was right that it was on the gallows.

I snatched a cap's worth of cloth from His coat,
and it covered my reason, my head, and
    my feet.

I pulled a thorn from the fence of his garden,
and it has not stopped working its way into
    my heart.

One morning a little of his wine
turned my heart into a lion hunter.
It's right that this separation he helped me feel
lurks like a monster within my heart.

Yet heaven's wild and unbroken colt
was trained by the hand of his love.
Though reason is learned and has its honors,
it pawned its cap and robes for a cup of love.

Many hearts have sought refuge from this love,
but it drags and pulls them to its own refuge.

One cold day a bearskin was floating
   down the river.
I said to a man who had no clothes,
"Jump in and pull it out."

But the bearskin was a live bear,
and the man who jumped in so eagerly
was caught in the clutches of what he went
   to grab.

"Let go of it," I said, "Fighting won't get you
   anywhere."
"Let go of it? This coat won't let go of me!"
Silence. Just a hint. Who needs volumes of
   stories?

And He Is with Us

Totally unexpected my guest arrived.
"Who is it?" asked my heart.
"The face of the moon," said my soul.

As he entered the house,
we all ran into the street madly
looking for the moon.
"I'm in here," he was calling from inside,
but we were calling him outside
unaware of his call.
Our drunken nightingale is singing in the
    garden,
and we are cooing like doves,
"Where, where, where?"

A crowd formed: "Where's the thief?"
And the thief among us was saying,
"Yeah, where's the thief?"
All our voices became mixed together
and not one voice stood out from the others.

And He is with you means
He is searching with you.
He is nearer to you than yourself.
Why look outside?

Become like melting snow;
wash yourself of yourself.
With love your inner voice will find a tongue
growing like a silent white lily in the heart.

You and I

A moment of happiness,
you and I sitting on the verandah,
apparently two, but one in soul, you and I.

We feel the flowing water of life here,
you and I, with the garden's beauty,
the birds singing.

The stars will be watching us,
and we will show them
how it is to be the thinnest crescent moon.

You and I, unselfed, will be together,
indifferent to idle speculation, you and I.
The parrots of heaven will be cracking sugar
as we laugh together, you and I.

And what is even more amazing
is that while here together, you and I
are at this very moment in Iraq and Khorasan.
In one form upon this earth,
and in another form in a timeless sweet land.

Search the Darkness

Sit with your friends; don't go back to sleep.
Don't sink like a fish to the bottom of the sea.

Surge like an ocean,
don't scatter yourself like a storm.

Life's waters flow from darkness.
Search the darkness, don't run from it.

Night travelers are full of light,
and you are, too; don't leave this
   companionship.

Be a wakeful candle in a golden dish,
don't slip into the dirt like quicksilver.

The moon appears for night travelers,
be watchful when the moon is full.

This Useless Heart

Heart, since you embraced the mysteries,
you have become useless for anything else.
Go mad, don't stay sane.
People meditate to get something.
All you do is give.
Crazy Majnun's priorities are now yours, too.

If you want to be respectable,
why do you go downtown drunk?
It's no good just sitting in some corner,
once you've made friends
with the dissolute of this path.

Go back to the desert;
leave this shabby town.
There's the smell of a tavern
somewhere in this neighborhood,
and it's already got you high.

Now follow it.
Go to Qaf Mountain like the Simurgh,
leave these owls and herons.
Go into the thicket of Reality like a lion.

Why linger with hyenas and dogs?
Don't go after the scent of Joseph's shirt,
like Jacob, his father,
you have already mourned his death

The Ruins of the Heart

I am a sculptor, a molder of form.
In every moment I shape an idol.
But then, in front of you, I melt them down.

I can rouse a hundred forms
and fill them with spirit,
but when I look into your face,
I want to throw them in the fire.

Do you merely fill this drunkard's glass,
or do you really oppose the sober?
Is it you who brings to ruin
every house I build?

My soul spills into yours and is blended.
Because my soul has absorbed your fragrance,
I cherish it.

Every drop of blood I spill
informs the earth,
"I merge with my Beloved
when I participate in love."

In this house of mud and water,
my heart has fallen into ruins.
Enter this house, my Love, or let me leave.

Because I Cannot Sleep

Because I cannot sleep
I make music at night.
I am troubled by the one
whose face has the color of spring flowers.
I have neither sleep nor patience,
neither a good reputation nor disgrace.

A thousand robes of wisdom are gone.
All my good manners have run a thousand
    miles away.

The heart and the mind
are left angry with each other.
The stars and the moon are envious of each
    other.
Because of this alienation the physical universe
is getting tighter and tighter.

The moon says, "How long will I remain
suspended without a sun?"
Without Love's jewel inside of me,
let the bazaar of my existence
be destroyed stone by stone.

O Love, You who have been called by a
   thousand names,
You who know how to pour the wine
into the chalice of the body,
You who give culture to a thousand cultures,
You who are faceless but have a thousand faces,
O Love, You who shape the faces
of Turks, Europeans, and Zanzibaris,
give me a glass from Your bottle,
or a handful of *bheng* from your branch.

Remove the cork once more.
Then we'll see a thousand chiefs prostrate,
and a circle of ecstatic troubadours will play.
Then the addict will be freed of craving.
and will be resurrected,
and stand in awe till Judgment Day.

Kabir Helminski with Lail Fouladvend

The Drunkards and the Tavern

I'm drunk and you're insane,
who's going to take us home?
How many times did they say,
"Drink just a little, only two or three at most?"

In this city no one I see is conscious;
one is worse off than the next,
frenzied and insane.

Dear one, come to the tavern of ruin
and experience the pleasures of the soul.
What happiness can there be apart
from this intimate conversation
with the Beloved, the Soul of souls?

In every corner there are drunkards,
    arm in arm,
while the Server pours the wine
from a royal decanter to every particle of being.

You belong to the tavern: your income is wine,
and wine is all you ever buy.
Don't give even a second away
to the concerns of the merely sober.

O lute player, are you more drunk, or am I?
In the presence of one as drunk as you,
  my magic is a myth.

When I went outside the house,
some drunk approached me,
and in his eyes I saw
hundreds of hidden gardens and sanctuaries.

Like a ship without an anchor,
he rocked this way and that.
Hundreds of intellectuals and wise men
could die from a taste of his yearning.

I asked, "Where are you from?"
He laughed and said, "O soul,
half of me is from Turkestan
and half from Farghana.

Half of me is water and mud, half heart and
  soul;
half of me is the ocean's shore, half is all pearl."

"Be my friend," I pleaded,
"I'm one of your family."
"I know the difference between family and
  outsiders."

I've neither a heart nor a turban,
and here in this house of hangovers
my breast is filled with unspoken words.
Shall I try to explain or not?

Have I lived among the lame for so long
that I've begun to limp myself?
And yet no slap of pain could disturb
a drunkenness like this.

Listen, can you hear a wail
arising from the pillar of grief?
Shams al-Haqq of Tabriz, where are you now,
after all the mischief you've stirred in our
        hearts?

K. Helminski, A. Godlas, and L. Saedian

Ramadan

O moon-faced Beloved,
the month of Ramadan has arrived.
Cover the table
and open the path of praise.

O fickle busy-body,
it's time to change your ways.
Can you see the one who's selling the halvah;
how long will it be the halvah you desire?

Just a glimpse of the halvah-maker
has made you so sweet even honey says
"I'll put myself beneath your feet, like soil;
I'll worship at your shrine."

Your chick frets within the egg
with all your eating and choking.
Break out of your shell
that your wings may grow.
Let yourself fly.

The lips of the Master are parched
from calling the Beloved.
The sound of your call resounds
through the horn of your empty belly.

Let nothing be inside of you.
Be empty: give your lips to the lips of the reed.
When like a reed you fill with His breath,
then you'll taste sweetness.

Sweetness is hidden in the Breath
that fills the reed.
Be like Mary—by that sweet breath
a child grew within her.

Nevit Ergin with Camille Helminski

With Us

Even if you're not a seeker,
still, follow us, keep searching with us.
Even if you don't know how
to play and sing,
you'll become like us;
with us you'll start singing and dancing.

Even if you are Qarun, the richest of kings,
when you fall in love,
you'll become a beggar.
Though you are a sultan, like us you'll become
   a slave.

One candle of this gathering
is worth a hundred candles; it's light is as great.
Either you are alive or dead.
You'll come back to life with us.

Unbind your feet.
Show the rose garden—
start laughing with your whole body,
like a rose, like us.

Put on the mantle for a moment
and see the ones whose hearts are alive.
Then, throw out your satin dresses
and cover yourself with a cloak, like us.

When a seed falls into the ground,
it germinates, grows, and becomes a tree:
if you understand these symbols,
you'll follow us, and fall to the ground, with us.

God's Shams of Tabriz says
to the heart's bud,
"If your eyes are opened,
you'll see the things worth seeing."

Nevit Ergin with Camille Helminski

Banners of Praise

Our fasting is over; it's the feast day of spring!
O dearest guest, welcome; sorrow be gone!
All praise be to God!

O Love once forsaken,
abandoned heart be forgotten now;
your Beloved has arrived, and will forever
    remain.
All praise be to God!

Parting is forever parted;
separation is severed at last;
union is united with no more delay:
All praise be to God!

Flight has flown and exile's pain is banished;
distance is now distant;
our nest is filled with joy:
All praise be to God!

The moon in the heavens, the rose in the heart,
in Love's garden,
the King in his palace, proud banners
    show forth:
All praise be to God!

Life stirs in the root hair;
fluid sap spreads in each tiny leaf;
green buds on the branches crown
   His dominion:
All praise be to God!

Let the despised enemy come,
for he'll meet our Defender;
we challenge his approach
for now in safety we say:
All praise be to God!

Flood me completely,
with the fire of Love's burning,
for now I can bear it and not burn away:
All praise be to God!

For now in certainty, my soul is free,
and all of earth's sadness
has dissolved in earth's clay.
All praise be to God!

O chalice overflowing,
poured out for these thirsty worlds—
we thank you, we bless you,
and drink while we pray:
All praise be to God!

The world lay parched for so long,
an open desert,
until the dew glistened, and your breath
came on the wings of morning.
All praise be to God!

As we waited we were longing for Spring's sun
to renew this life of ours.
Today, Jalâluddin's warm breath
arrived from the East.
All praise be to God!

Camille Helminski with William Hastie

This Bewildering Game

How are you? *How are you?*
Neither "how" nor "what" will understand you.
Except for the Sultan, the one who is beyond
    "how" and "what,"
no one will be able to understand.

O my Beauty, the universe is illumined by
    You—
filled with light.
Yet neither the sky nor the earth can see it fully.

A wind moves this blue curtain
but it's not the air blowing through;
it's a wind known only by God.

Do you know who stitches that cloak of joy,
that cloak of grief?
Why does this cloak
think himself different than the one who sews?

Do you know what image shines
in the mirror's heart?
The one who knows
is the one whose heart is pure.

This universe is a banner
that keeps fluttering.
Your heart sees the banner;
your soul thinks it's the air that makes it move.

But the one who knows
how helpless air is
recognizes that everything
is nothing but God.

O God's Shams of Tabriz,
Our Lord has so many tricks up His sleeve;
without your dice, how could the soul
even begin to play this bewildering
    backgammon game?

Nevit Ergin and Camille Helminski

Water and Wine

With Your sweet Soul, this soul of mine
has merged as water does with wine.
Who can part the water from the wine,
or me from You when we combine?

You have become my greater self;
how can smallness limit me?
You've taken on my being,
how shall I not take on Yours?

Forever, You have claimed me
that forever I may know You're mine.
Your love has pierced me to the depths,
its ecstasy entwines both bone and nerve.

I rest as a *ney** laid upon Your lips;
as an *oud*† I lie against Your breast.
Breathe deeply in me that I may sigh;
Strike upon my strings and tears glisten.

*Reed flute.
†Ancestor of the flute.

Sweet are my tears and sweet my sighs;
worldly joys I return to the world.
You remain in my inmost Soul
whose depths the mirrored heavens reflect.

O pearl in this mussel shell:
O diamond in my darkest mine!
In You, this honey is dissolved,
O milk of life, so mild, so fine!

Our sweetnesses, all merged in You,
sweeten infant smiles.
You crush me into rose oil, drop by drop;
nor do I complain beneath the press.

In Your sweet pain, pain dissolves;
for I, Your rose, had this intent.
You bade me blossom on Your robe,
and made me for all eyes Your sign.

And when You pour me upon this world,
it blooms in Beauty, fully Divine.

Camille Helminski with William Hastie

Be Love's Willing Slave

Come and be Love's willing slave,
for Love's slavery will save you.
Forsake the slavery of this world
and take up Love's sweet service.
The free, the world enslaves,
but to slaves Love grants freedom.
I crave release from this world
like a bird from its egg;
free me from this shell that clings.
As from the grave, grant me new life.
O Love, O quail in the free fields of spring,
wildly sing songs of joy.

Camille Helminski with William Hastie

Intellect Is a Shackle

O my child, intellect is a shackle
on the foot of one who walks the Path.
Break the bond; the Way is open!
The intellect is a chain, the heart may be
    deceptive,
and even your soul is a veil—
the Path is hidden from all three.

When you lift the intellect, soul, and heart,
the station of nearness you reach is still
    subjective.
One who gets lost isn't considered brave.
Love takes aim at the one who has no troubles.
Know that the arrow of the Friend is ready
    in the bow.
Make your chest a target in front of it.

Love isn't the work of the tender and the gentle;
Love is the work of wrestlers.
The one who becomes a servant of lovers
is really a fortunate sovereign.
Don't ask anyone about Love;
ask Love alone about Love.
Love is a cloud that scatters pearls.

Love doesn't need me to translate; it translates
   for itself.
If you journey to the seventh heaven,
Love is a useful ladder.
Wherever a caravan journeys, Love is its
   *qiblah**
May this universe not deceive you,
waylaying you from Love,
for this universe comes from you.
Let's go! Close your mouth like mother of pearl.

Be silent, for this tongue of yours
is the enemy of the soul.
O child, Shams of Tabriz has arrived;
the soul is full of joy
for the time has come to join in union with his
   sun.

Refik Algan and Camille Helminski

---

*The direction or orientation for prayer, more usu-
ally Mecca.

The Funny Thing Is . . .

When I want to leave
You hold my feet and won't let me go.
You steal my heart,
and sit on top of it.

Because of the secret You whispered,
and the moon You revealed,
Love's wind whirls in my head
and my heart loses its hands and feet.

You pass many nights in vigil,
and soar across this sky-dome with the
    wings of fasting,
in love with flight.

You saw me lost, waving and crying,
and said, "I am the guide.
I'll show you the road
for which you have been searching."

I'm hidden behind the wall,
and yet I'm right beside you.
You are oppressed and suffering,
yet I am near.

You who are anxious to get
where you think you're going,
I'll make your dreams come true.
I'll cook well every pot you try to boil.

My friend, you thought you lost Him;
that all your life you've been separated
    from Him.
Filled with wonder,
you've always looked outside for Him,
and haven't searched within your own house.

The funny part is
that in this search,
Beauty has always accompanied you.
Wherever you have been,
He is the One holding your hand.

Keep looking for Him with Him;
You and He are on the same road.
O Beloved, You're so obvious
You're hidden from sight!

Camille and Kabir Helminski with Nevit Ergin

When Sand Suffices

When you have no cleansing water,
sand suffices—
the Prophet gave this rule to those in need,
and still it continues.

Do you know why, O faithful ones?
Listen to the truth the wise reveal—
often in the desert, water is unseen,
but for the traveler sand abounds.

From the desert I will guide
the one who calls me guide
to the place where living waters flow,
to the Garden Love encompasses.

There, bathe in abundance,
drought dispelled,
for once you've washed in that stream,
the need for sand disappears;

Freed of any method,
purely by Spirit you'll be ruled.
O Master! Your exalted soul has seen
the Truth through every veil.

Camille Helminski with William Hastie

Who Are You and What Do You Want?

He said, "Who is at the door?"
I said, "Your humble slave."
He said, "Why have you come?"
I said, "To offer salaams."
He said, "How long will you wait?"
I said, "Until you call."
He said, "How long will you boil?"
I said, "Until you resurrect me."

I laid claim to love, swore oaths of love,
and told how I lost all power and position
   for love.
He said, "The judge asks to see your witness."
"These tears, these pale cheeks."
"Your witness has blood-shot eyes and cannot
   be trusted."
I said, "By your high justice, they are just
   and true."
He said, "Who was your companion?"
"Your gift of imaginal vision."
"What called you here?"
"The fragrance of your cup."

"What do you want?"
"Faithfulness and intimacy."
"What do you want from me?" He said.
"Your subtle grace," I said.
"Where is the greatest pleasure?"
"In Caesar's palace," I said.
"And what did you see there?"
"A hundred fascinations."
He said, "Then why is it so desolate?"
"For fear of thieves."
"Who is the thief?" He said?
"Whatever challenges our vanity," I said.
"Where is safety?" he said.
"In abstinence and pure consciousness
   of God."
"What is abstinence?"
I said, "The way of peace."
"Where is catastrophe?"
"In the street of Your love."
"How do you travel there?" He asked.
"With integrity," I said.
Silence. If I were to utter more,
you would be completely gone.
left without a door or roof.

To Take a Step without Feet

This is love: to fly toward a secret sky,
to cause a hundred veils to fall each moment.
First, to let go of life.
In the end, to take a step without feet.
To regard this world as invisible,
and to disregard what appears to the self.

Heart, I said, what a gift it has been
to enter this circle of lovers,
to see beyond seeing itself,
to reach and feel within the breast.

My soul, where does this breathing arise?
How does this beating heart exist?
Bird of the soul, speak in your own words,
and I will understand.

The heart replied: I was in the workplace
the day this house of water and clay was fired.
I was already fleeing that created house,
even as it was being created.
When I could no longer resist, I was dragged down,
and my features were molded from a handful
  of earth.

This Body Is a Rose

Each form you see has its unseen archetype.
If the form is transient, its essence is eternal.
If you have known beauty in a face
or wisdom in a word,
let this counsel your heart:
what perishes is not real.

Since the springhead is timeless,
its branches refresh.
Since neither can cease,
what is the cause of your sorrow?

Think of the soul as source
and created things as springs.
While the source exists,
the springs continually flow.

Empty your head of grief
and drink from the stream.
Don't think of it failing —
this water is endless.

From the moment you came into
   the manifest world,
a ladder was offered for your escape.
From mineral substance you became
   a living plant,
and later a roving animal. Is this a secret?

Afterwards, as a human being,
you developed reason, consciousness, faith.
See how this body has risen from the dust like
   a rose?

When you have surpassed the human state,
your angelic nature will unfold
in a world beyond this world.
Surpass the angels then and enter the Sea.

Your drop will merge with a hundred Seas
   of Oman.
Let go of him you called "son,"
and say "One" with your life.
Although your body has aged,
your soul has become young.

Empty the Glass of Your Desire

Join yourself to friends
and know the joy of the soul.
Enter the neighborhood of ruin
with those who drink to the dregs.

Empty the glass of your desire
so that you won't be disgraced.
Stop looking for something out there
and begin seeing within.

Open your arms if you want an embrace.
Break the earthen idols and release the
     radiance.
Why get involved with a hag like this world?
You know what it will cost.

And three pitiful meals a day
is all that weapons and violence can earn.
At night when the Beloved comes
will you be nodding on opium?

If you close your mouth to food,
you can know a sweeter taste.
Our Host is no tyrant. We gather in a circle.
Sit down with us beyond the wheel of time.

Here is the deal: give one life
and receive a hundred.
Stop growling like dogs,
and know the shepherd's care.

You keep complaining about others
and all they owe you?
Well, forget about them;
just be in His presence.
When the earth is this wide,
why are you asleep in a prison?
Think of nothing but the source of thought.
Feed the soul; let the body fast.

Avoid knotted ideas;
untie yourself in a higher world.
Limit your talk
for the sake of timeless communion.

Abandon life and the world,
and find the life *of* the world.

That Which Has No Clue

At the last you vanished, gone to the Unseen.
Strange the path you took out of this world.
Strange how your beating wings
    demolished the cage,
and you flew away to the world of the soul.

You were some old woman's favorite falcon,
but when you heard the falcon drum,
you escaped to the placeless.

You were a drunken nightingale among owls,
but when the scent of the rose-garden reached
    you,
you were gone.

The bitter wine you drank with us left its
    headache,
but at last you entered a timeless tavern.
Like an arrow you went straight for the target of
    bliss,
straight to the mark like an arrow from a bow.

Like a ghoul, the world tried to deceive you
with its false clues, but you refused the clues,
and went straight to that which had no clue.

Now that you are the sun, what good is a crown?
And how do you tie your belt,
now that you've vanished from the middle?

Heart, what a rare bird you are,
that in your yearning for heaven's attention,
you flew to the spear-point like a shield!

The rose flees autumn,
but what a foolhardy rose you are,
seeking the autumn wind.

You were rain from another world
that fell on this dusty earth.
You ran in all directions
and escaped down the gutter.

Be silent. Be free
of the pain of speech.
Don't sleep, since you took refuge
with so loving a Friend.

3

SELECTIONS
FROM THE
MATHNAWI

Kabir and Camille Helminski

Song of the Reed*

Listen to the reed and the tale it tells,
how it sings of separation:
Ever since they cut me from the reed bed,
my wail has caused men and women to weep.
I want a heart torn open with longing
to share the pain of this love.
Whoever has been parted from his source
longs to return to that state of union.
At every gathering I play my lament.
I'm a friend to both happy and sad.
Each befriended me for his own reasons,
yet none searched out the secrets I contain.
My secret is not different than my lament,
yet this is not for the senses to perceive.
The body is not hidden from the soul,
nor is the soul hidden from the body,
and yet the soul is not for everyone to see.
This flute is played with fire, not with wind,
and without this fire you would not exist.
It is the fire of love that inspires the flute.

*All translations in this chapter are by Kabir and
Camille Helminski except as noted.

It is the ferment of love that completes
   the wine.
The reed is a comfort to all estranged lovers.
Its music tears our veils away. Have you
ever seen a poison or antidote like the reed?
Have you seen a more intimate companion
   and lover?
It sings of the path of blood;
it relates the passion of Majnun.
Only to the senseless is this sense confided.
Does the tongue have any patron but the ear?
Our days grow more unseasonable,
these days which mix with grief and pain . . .
but if the days that remain are few,
let them go; it doesn't matter. But You,
   You remain,
for nothing is as pure as You are.
All but the fish quickly have their fill of His
   water;
and the day is long without His daily bread.
The raw do not understand the state of the ripe,
so my words will be brief.

Break your bonds, be free, my child!
How long will silver and gold enslave you?
If you pour the whole sea into a jug,
will it hold more than one day's store?
The greedy eye, like the jug, is never filled.
Until content, the oyster holds no pearl.
Only one who has been undressed by Love
is free of defect and desire.
O Gladness, O Love, our partner in trade,
healer of all our ills, our Plato and Galen,
remedy of our pride and our vanity.
With love this earthly body could soar in the
     air;
the mountain could arise and nimbly dance.
Love gave life to Mount Sinai, O lover.
Sinai was drunk; Moses lost consciousness.
Pressed to the lips of one in harmony with
     myself,
I might also tell all that can be told;
but without a common tongue, I am dumb,
even if I have a hundred songs to sing.
When the rose is gone and the garden faded,
you will no longer hear the nightingale's song.
The Beloved is all; the lover just a veil.
The Beloved is living; the lover a dead thing.

If Love withholds its strengthening care,
the lover is left like a bird without wings.
How will I be awake and aware
if the light of the Beloved is absent?
Love wills that this Word be brought forth.
If you find the mirror of the heart dull,
the rust has not been cleared from its face.
O friends, listen to this tale,
the marrow of our inward state.

Kabir Helminski
MATHNAWI I, 1–35

When a Man and a Woman Become One

I darkened my eyes
with the dust of sadness
until each of them was a sea full of pearls.

All the tears which we creatures shed for Him
are not tears as many think but pearls. . . .

I am complaining about the Soul of the soul,
but I'm no complainer; I'm simply saying
    how it is.

My heart tells me it is distressed with Him,
but I can only laugh at such pretended injuries.

Be fair, You who are the Glory of the just.
You, Soul, free of "we" and "I,"
subtle spirit within each man and woman.

When a man and a woman become one,
that "one" is You.
And when that one is obliterated, there You are.

Where is this "we" and this "I"?
By the side of the Beloved.
You made this "we" and this "I"
in order that you might play

this game of courtship with Yourself,
that all "you's" and "I's" might become
    one soul
and finally drown in the Beloved.

All this is true. Come!
You who are the Creative Word: *Be.*
You, so far beyond description.

Is it possible for the bodily eye to see You?
Can thought comprehend Your laughter
    or grief?
Tell me now, can it possibly see You at all?
Such a heart has only borrowed things
    to live with.

The garden of love is green without limit
and yields many fruits other than sorrow or joy.
Love is beyond either condition:
without spring, without autumn, it is always
    fresh.

Kabir Helminski
MATHNAWI I, 1779–94

Companionship with the Holy

Don't take a wooden sword into battle.
Go, find one of steel;
then march forward with joy.

The saint's protection is Truth's sword:
your time with him
is worth as much as the cup of life itself.

All the wise have said the same:
the one who knows God
is God's mercy to His creatures . . .

Companionship with the holy makes you one
of them.
Though you're rock or marble, you'll become
a jewel
when you reach the man of heart.

Plant the love of the holy ones within your
spirit;
don't give your heart to anything,
but the love of those whose hearts are glad.

Don't go to the neighborhood of despair:
there is hope.
Don't go in the direction of darkness:
suns exist.

MATHNAWI I, 714–17, 721–24

The Tongue

O tongue, you are an endless treasure.
O tongue, you are also an endless disease.

MATHNAWI I, 1702

I Am Burning

I am burning.
If any one lacks tinder,
let him set his rubbish ablaze with my fire.

MATHNAWI I, 1721

Drowned in God

Dam the torrent of ecstasy when it runs in flood,
so that it won't bring shame and ruin.
But why should I fear ruin?
Under the ruin waits a royal treasure.
He that is drowned in God wishes to be more
    drowned.
While his spirit is tossed up and down
by the waves of the sea,
he asks, "Is the bottom of the sea more
    delightful, or the top?
Is the Beloved's arrow more fascinating,
    or the shield?"
O heart, if you recognize any difference
between joy and sorrow,
these lies will tear you apart.
Although your desire tastes sweet,
doesn't the Beloved desire you
to be desireless?
The life of lovers is in death:
you will not win the Beloved's heart
unless you lose your own.

MATHNAWI I, 1743–49, 1751

Flattery

The world's flattery and hypocrisy
is a sweet morsel:
eat less of it, for it is full of fire.
Its fire is hidden while its taste is manifest,
but its smoke becomes visible in the end.

MATHNAWI I, 1855–56

Counting Out Gold Coins

God gave me a life,
the value of every single day
He alone knows.
I have spent my life, breath by breath,
singing my songs,
so consumed by the melody and beat
I forgot the moment of bitter departure.
While I sang my fluid tunes
the seed of my heart dried up,
the caravan passed, the day grew late.
O God, help me against this self of mine
that is seeking help from You;
I seek justice from no one but from
this justice-seeking self.

I shall not get justice from any one
except from Him
who is nearer to me than myself;

For this I-ness comes
moment by moment from Him,
and when it no longer remains
I see only Him, counting out gold coins,
and I forget myself,
because I cannot take my eyes off of Him.

MATHNAWI I, 2195–98

Surrender

It suits the generous man to give money,
but truly the generosity of the lover
is to surrender his soul.
If you give bread for God's sake,
you will be given bread in return;
if you give your life for God's sake,
you will be given Life in return.

MATHNAWI I, 2235–36

Woman Is a Ray of God

Muhammad said,
"Woman prevails over the wise and intelligent;
while the ignorant dominate over her."
They lack tenderness and affection
because their animality prevails.
Love and gentleness are human qualities;
aggressiveness and lust are bestial.
Woman is a ray of God.
She is not that earthly beloved.
You could say:
she is creative, not created.

MATHNAWI I, 2433–37

The Gifts of Lovers

If a spiritual explanation alone were sufficient,
the creation of the world
would have been vain and pointless.
If love were only spiritual,
the practices of fasting and worship
would not exist.
The gifts of lovers to one another are,
in respect to love, nothing but forms;
yet, they testify
to an invisible love.

MATHNAWI I, 2625–27

The Master Imbues His Specialty

Whatever knowledge the master
is known to have,
with it the souls of his pupils are imbued:
The theologian imbues with theology;
the master of law with jurisprudence.
The master who is absorbed in the Way
will help the seeker become absorbed in God.
Of all the things to know,
the best preparation and provision on the day
    of death
is the knowledge of spiritual poverty.

MATHNAWI I, 2829–34

Fasting

Fast from thoughts, fast:
thoughts are like the lion and the wild ass;
men's hearts are the thickets they haunt.
Fasting is the first principle of health;
restraint is superior to medication;
scratching only aggravates the itch.
Fast, and behold the strength of the spirit.

MATHNAWI I, 2909–11

Polish

If you are irritated by every rub,
how will your mirror be polished?

MATHNAWI I, 2980

The Spiritual Surgeon

Can the water of a polluted stream
clear out the dung?
Can human knowledge sweep away
the ignorance of the sensual self?
How does a sword fashion its own hilt?
Go, entrust the cure of this wound to a surgeon,
for flies will gather around the wound
until it can't be seen.
These are your selfish thoughts
and all you dream of owning.
The wound is your own dark hole.

MATHNAWI I, 3221–24

Loving to Forgive

Be cheerful, call for help
to the One who comes at the call,
saying, "Forgive us, You who *love* to forgive."

MATHNAWI I, 3252–53

The Pearl

Everyone is so afraid of death,
but the real Sufis just laugh:
nothing tyrannizes their hearts.
What strikes the oyster shell
doesn't damage the pearl.

MATHNAWI I, 3495–96

Draw Near

Whatever it is you wish to marry,
Go, absorb yourself in that beloved,
assume its shape and qualities.
If you wish for the light, prepare yourself
to receive it; if you wish to be far from God,
nourish your egoism and drive yourself away.
If you wish to find a way out of this ruined
    prison,
don't turn your head away from the Beloved,
but *bow in worship and draw near*.

MATHNAWI I, 3605–07

The Embryo

When the time comes for the embryo
to receive the spirit of life,
at that time the sun begins to help.
This embryo is brought into movement,
for the sun quickens it with spirit.

From the other stars this embryo
received only an impression,
until the sun shone upon it.
How did it become connected
with the shining sun
in the womb?

By ways hidden from our senses:
the way whereby gold is nourished,
the way a common stone becomes a garnet
and the ruby red,
the way fruit is ripened,
and the way courage comes
to one distraught
with fear.

MATHNAWI 1, 3775–82

The Darkness

Night cancels the business of the day;
inertia recharges the mind.
Then the day cancels the night,
and inertia disappears in the light.
Though we sleep and rest in the dark,
doesn't the dark contain the water of life?
Be refreshed in the darkness.
Doesn't a moment of silence
restore beauty to the voice?
Opposites manifest through opposites:
in the black core of the heart
God created the eternal light of love.

MATHNAWI I, 3861–65

Permission to Destroy

He alone has the right to break,
for He alone has the power to mend.
He that knows how to sew together,
knows how to tear apart:
whatever He sells,
He buys something better in exchange.
He lays the house in ruins;
then in a moment He makes it
more livable than before.

MATHNAWI I, 3882–86

Sunlight fell upon the wall;
the wall received a borrowed splendor.
Why set your heart on a piece of earth,
O simple one? Seek out the source
which shines forever.

MATHNAWI II, 708–09

Pearl of the Heart

On the back of the donkey
are the goods and the money;
but the pearl of your heart
is the investment which supports
a hundred donkeys.

MATHNAWI II, 726

The Fire the Dervish Needs

The fire that iron or gold needs—
would it be good for fresh quinces and apples?
The apple and quince are just slightly raw;
unlike iron, they need only a gentle heat.
But gentle flames are not enough for iron;
it eagerly draws to itself the fiery dragon's
    breath.
That iron is the dervish who bears hardship:
under the hammer and fire, he happily
    glows red.

MATHNAWI II, 827–30

Substance

You think the shadow is the substance:
so to you the *substance*
has become a cheap toy.
Wait until the day when that substance
freely unfolds its wings.
Then you will see the mountains
become as soft as wool,
and this earth of heat and ice
become as nothing;
you will see neither the sky nor the stars,
nor any existence but God—
the One, the Living, the Loving.

MATHNAWI II, 1042–45

The Soul Garden

Just as the heart becomes carefree
in a place of green, growing plants,
goodwill and kindness are born
when our souls enter happiness.

MATHNAWI II, 1095–96

Light upon Light

The sensuous eye is a horse;
the light of God is the rider:
without the rider the horse is useless.
The light of God rides the body's eye.
The soul yearns for God.
God's light enhances the senses.
This is the meaning of *Light upon Light*.

MATHNAWI II, 1286, 1290–93

The Invisible Hand

See how the hand is invisible while the pen
   is writing;
the horse careening, yet the rider unseen;
the arrow flying, but the bow out of sight;
individual souls existing,
while the Soul of souls is hidden.

MATHNAWI II, 1303–04

Mature Yourself

No mirror ever became iron again;
no bread ever became wheat;
no ripened grape ever became sour fruit.
Mature yourself and be secure
from a change for the worse.
Become Light.

MATHNAWI II, 1317–18

Be Washed

Water says to the dirty, "Come here."
The dirty one says, "I am so ashamed."
Water says, "How will your shame
be washed away
without me?"

MATHNAWI II, 1366–67

Love's Furnace

My soul is a furnace
happy with the fire.
Love, too, is a furnace,
and ego its fuel.

MATHNAWI II, 1376–77

Pure Gold

How will you know your real friends?
Pain is as dear to them as life.
A friend is like gold. Trouble is like fire.
Pure gold delights in the fire.

MATHNAWI II, 1458; 1461

The Thief Will Enter

No matter what plans you make,
no matter what you acquire,
the thief will enter from the unguarded side.
Be occupied, then, with what you really value
and let the thief take something less.

MATHNAWI II, 1505–07

The Mysteries

The unsuspecting child first wipes the tablet
and then writes the letters on it.
God turns the heart into blood and desperate
    tears;
then He writes the spiritual mysteries on it.

MATHNAWI II, 1826–27

The Truth of Things

The porter runs to the heavy load
and takes it from others,
knowing burdens are the foundation of ease
and bitter things are the forerunners of
    pleasure.
See how the porters struggle over the load!
It's the way of those who see the truth of things.

MATHNAWI II, 1834–36

Make Yourself Low

Loving-kindness is drawn to the saint,
as medicine is drawn
to the pain it must cure.
Where there is pain, the remedy follows:
wherever the lowlands are, the water goes.
If you want the water of mercy,
    make yourself low;
then drink the wine of mercy and be drunk.
Mercy upon mercy rises to your head
    like a flood.
Don't settle on a single mercy, O son.
Bring the sky beneath your feet
and listen to celestial music everywhere.

MATHNAWI II, 1938–42

That Treasure Could Be Anybody

You may despair of finding
a true friend of God;
but since the treasure does exist in this world,
consider no ruin empty of treasure.
Go to every dervish at random,
and when you find the sign of a true saint,
keep his company regularly.
If the inner eye has not been granted to you,
always think that treasure could be in anybody.

MATHNAWI II, 2153–55

To Clutch at Madness

Conventional opinion is the ruin of our souls,
something borrowed which we mistake as our
    own.
Ignorance is better than this; clutch at madness
    instead.
Always run from what seems to benefit your self:
sip the poison and spill the water of life.
Revile those who flatter you;
lend both interest and principal to the poor.
Let security go and be at home amid dangers.
Leave your good name behind
    and accept disgrace.
I have lived with cautious thinking;
Now I'll make myself mad.

MATHNAWI II, 2327–32

Your Mysterious Giving

O Lord, truly, Your grace is not from our work,
but from Your mysterious giving.
Save us from what our own hands might do;
lift the veil, but do not tear it.
Save us from the ego; its knife has
    reached our bones.
Who but You will break these chains?
Let us turn from ourselves to You
Who are nearer to us than ourselves.
Even this prayer is Your gift to us.
How else has a rose garden grown
    from these ashes?

MATHNAWI II, 2443–49

Pain That Saves

Delusion is a Divine curse
that makes someone envious, conceited,
   malicious,
so that he doesn't know the evil he does
will strike him back.
If he could see his nothingness
and his deadly, festering wound,
pain would arise from looking within,
and that pain would save him.

MATHNAWI II, 2513–17

Willingly, or Unwillingly

The faithful bow willingly,
intending the pleasure of God.
The unbeliever worships God, but unwillingly,
intending some other desire.
Yes, he keeps the King's fortress in good repair,
but claims to be in command.

MATHNAWI II, 2544–46

The Most Useful Trade

In this world you have become affluent
    and well dressed,
but when you come out of this world,
how will you be?
Learn a trade that will earn you forgiveness.
In the world beyond there's also traffic and
    trade.
Beside those earnings, this world is just play.
Just as children embrace in fantasy intercourse,
or set up their own candy shop,
this world is a game.
Night falls, and the child
comes home hungry, without his friends.

MATHNAWI II, 2593–99

The Touchstone

Iblis asked, "Can you tell a lie from the truth,
you who are filled with illusion?"
Muawiya answered,
"The Prophet has given a clue,
a touchstone to know
the base coin from the true.
He has said, 'That which is false troubles
   the heart,
but Truth brings joyous tranquility.'"

MATHNAWI II, 2732–34

The Glow

Everyone who delights in some act of devotion
can't bear to miss it,
even for a short while.
That disappointment and grief
are worth a hundred prayers.
What is a formal prayer compared
to the glow of humble longing?

MATHNAWI II, 2769–70

Excuses

Someone says, "I can't help feeding my family.
I have to work so hard to earn a living."
He can do without God,
but not without food;
he can do without Religion,
but not without idols.
Where is one who'll say,
"If I eat bread without awareness of God,
I will choke."

MATHNAWI II, 3071–79

The Armor of Selflessness

If you put on the armor of a warrior,
yet are unable to defend yourself, you'll die.
Make your soul a shield,
bear what God sends you,
put down the sword.
Whoever is headless saves his head;
the selfless cannot be struck.
Those weapons are your selfish strategy,
the defense that wounds your own soul.

MATHNAWI II, 3169–71

Increase Your Need

The mouse-soul is nothing but a nibbler.
To the mouse is given a mind
proportionate to its need,
for without need, the All-Powerful
doesn't give anything to anyone.
Need, then, is the net for all things that exist:
A person has tools in proportion to his need.
So, quickly, increase your need, needy one,
that the sea of abundance
may surge up in loving-kindness.

MATHNAWI II, 3279–80; 3292

Essence and Form

The word is like the nest,
and meaning is the bird:
the body is the riverbed,
and spirit, the rolling water.

MATHNAWI II, 3293

The Path

The Path of Dervishhood
is not for the sake of avoiding
entanglement with the world.
No, it's because nothing exists but God.

MATHNAWI II, 3497

The Juice

A brotherhood is as a cluster of grapes:
When you squeeze them
they become one juice.
The unripe and the ripe are in opposition,
but when the immature ripens, too,
it becomes a close friend.

The hearty unripe grapes,
destined for ripening,
will at last become one in heart
by the breath of the masters of heart.

They grow rapidly to grapehood,
shedding duality and hatred and strife.
Then in maturity, they rend their skins,
till they become one.

MATHNAWI II, 3717–19, 3723–24

Sacred Work

Don't strive so much to complete your worldly
   affairs;
don't strive in any affair that's not sacred.

Otherwise at the end, you'll leave incomplete,
your spiritual affairs damaged and your bread
   unbaked.

The beautifying of your grave isn't done
by means of wood and stone and plaster;

no, but by digging your grave in spiritual purity
and burying your own selfhood in His,

and by becoming His dust, buried in love of
   Him,
so that from His breath, yours may be
   replenished.

MATHNAWI III, 128–32

Apprenticeship

If anybody goes traveling without a guide,
every two days' journey
becomes a journey of a hundred years.
The one who takes up a profession
without having had a teacher
becomes a laughingstock,
no matter where he lives.
Except perhaps for a single occurrence,
in all the world, is a descendant of Adam
ever born without parents?
The one who earns gains wealth;
it's a rare event
to find a buried treasure.

MATHNAWI III, 588; 590–92

Catch the Scent

Whether one moves slowly or with speed,
the one who is a seeker will be a finder.
Always seek with your whole self,
for the search is an excellent guide on the way.
Though you are lame and limping,
though your figure is bent and clumsy,
always creep towards the One.
Make that One your quest.
By speech and by silence and by fragrance,
catch the scent of the King everywhere.

MATHNAWI III, 978–81

The Hiding Place

The most secure place to hide a treasure of gold
is in some desolate, unnoticed place.
Why would anyone hide treasure
in plain sight?
And so it is said,
"Joy is hidden beneath sorrow."

MATHNAWI III, 1133–34

The Water of the Water

Day and night there is movement of foam on
    the Sea.
You see the foam, but not the Sea. Amazing!
We are dashing against each other like boats:
our eyes are darkened though we're in clear
    water.
O you who've gone to sleep in the body's boat,
you've seen the water,
but look at the Water of the water.
The water has a Water that is driving it;
the spirit has a Spirit that is calling it.

MATHNAWI III, 1271–74

Ripened Fruit

This world is like a tree,
and we are the half-ripe fruit upon it.
Unripe fruit clings tight to the branch
because, immature, it's not ready for the palace.
When fruits become ripe, sweet and juicy,
then biting their lips, they loosen their hold.
When the mouth has been sweetened by
    felicity,
the kingdom of the world loses its appeal.
To be tightly attached to the world signifies
    immaturity;
as long as you're an embryo,
blood-drinking is your business.

MATHNAWI III, 1293–97

Kernel and Shell

When the kernel swells the walnut shell,
or the pistachio, or the almond, the husk
    diminishes.
As the kernel of knowledge grows,
the husk thins and disappears,
because the lover is consumed by the Beloved.

Since the quality of being sought
is the opposite of seeking,
revelation and divine lightning
consume the prophet with fire.
When the attributes of the Eternal shine forth,
the cloak of temporality is burned away.

MATHNAWI III, 1388–91

The Lord of States

"I am only the house of your beloved,
not the beloved herself:
true love is for the treasure,
not for the coffer that contains it."
The real beloved is that one who is unique,
who is your beginning and your end.
When you find that one,
you'll no longer expect anything else:
that one is both the manifest and the mystery.
That one is the lord of states of feeling,
dependent on none:
month and year are slaves to that moon.
When He bids the "state,"
it does His bidding;
when that one wills, bodies become spirit.

MATHNAWI III, 1417–21

The Search

Even though you're not equipped,
keep searching:
equipment isn't necessary on the way
    to the Lord.
Whoever you see engaged in search,
become her friend and cast your head in front
    of her,
for choosing to be a neighbor of seekers,
you become one yourself;
protected by conquerors,
you will yourself learn to conquer.
If an ant seeks the rank of Solomon,
don't smile contemptuously upon its quest.
And of all your skills, and wealth and
    handicraft,
Weren't they first merely a thought and a quest?

MATHNAWI III, 1445–49

Your Demands

O You who make demands within me
    like an embryo,
since You are the one who makes the demand,
make its fulfillment easy;
show the way, help me,
or else relinquish Your claim
and take this burden from me!
Since from a debtor You're demanding gold,
give him gold in secret, O rich King!

MATHNAWI III, 1490–92

Beyond Appearances

Everyone can distinguish mercy from wrath,
whether he is wise or ignorant or corrupt,
but a mercy hidden in wrath,
or wrath hidden in the heart of mercy
can only be recognized by one whose heart
contains a spiritual touchstone.

MATHNAWI III, 1506–08

The Garment

When a man is busy in earnest,
he is unconscious of his pain.
I mention this insensibility to pain
so you may know how
the body resembles a garment.
Go, seek the one who wears it;
don't kiss a piece of cloth.

MATHNAWI III, 1610

Unfold Your Wings

Just as staying home is easy for some,
traveling comes easily to others.
Each of us was made for some particular work,
and the desire for that work
has been placed in our hearts.
How should hand and foot
be set in motion without desire?
If you see your desire leading toward Heaven,
unfold your wings to claim it;
but if you see your desire bends to the earth,
keep lamenting.
The wise weep in the beginning;
the foolish beat their heads at the end.
Discern the end from the beginning
so that you may not be repenting
when the Day of Reckoning arrives.

MATHNAWI III, 1616–23

Don't Linger

By God, don't linger
in any spiritual benefit you have gained,
but yearn for more—like one suffering
    from illness
whose thirst for water is never quenched.
This Divine Court is the Plane of the Infinite.
Leave the seat of honor behind;
let the Way be your seat of honor.

MATHNAWI III, 1960–61

Wings of Desire

People are distracted by objects of desire,
and afterwards repent of the lust they've
    indulged,
because they have indulged with a phantom
and are left even farther from Reality
    than before.
Your desire for the illusory is a wing,
by means of which a seeker might ascend to
    Reality.
When you have indulged a lust, your wing
    drops off;
you become lame and that fantasy flees.
Preserve the wing and don't indulge such lust,
so that the wing of desire may bear you to
    Paradise.
People fancy they are enjoying themselves,
but they are really tearing out their wings
for the sake of an illusion.

MATHNAWI III, 2133–38

How Have You Spent Your Life?

On Resurrection Day God will ask,
"During this reprieve I gave you,
what have you produced for Me?
Through what work have you reached your
   life's end?
For what end have your food
and your strength been consumed?
Where have you dimmed the luster of your eye?
Where have you dissipated your five senses?
You have spent your seeing, hearing,
   intelligence
and the pure celestial substances;
what have you purchased from the earth?
I gave you hands and feet as spade and mattock
for tilling the soil of good works;
when did they by themselves become existent?"

MATHNAWI III, 2149–53

The Window of the Soul

During prayer I often turn to God
and recall the meaning of the words of the
    Tradition,
"the delight felt in the ritual prayer."*
The window of my soul opens,
and from the purity of the unseen world,
the book of God comes to me directly.
The book, the rain of divine grace, and the light
are falling into my house through a window
from my real and original source.
The house without a window is hell;
to make a window is the essence of real religion.
Don't thrust your ax upon every thicket.
Come, use your ax to cut open a window.

MATHNAWI III, 2401–05

*The Prophet Muhammad (peace and blessings be
upon him) is said to have mentioned this as one of
the three things he loved best in the world.

The Companionship of Fools

Flee from the foolish; even Jesus
    fled from them.
Much blood has been shed
by companionship with fools!
Air absorbs water little by little;
even so, the fool drains you of spirit.
He steals your heat and leaves you cold,
like one who puts a stone beneath you.
The flight of Jesus wasn't caused by fear,
for he is safe from the mischief of fools;
his purpose was to teach by example.

MATHNAWI III, 2595–98

The Essence of All Sciences

If you know the value of every article of
    merchandise,
but you don't know the value of your own soul,
it will all have been pointless.
You've come to know the fortunate
and the inauspicious stars,
but you don't know whether you yourself
are fortunate or unlucky.
This, this is the essence of all sciences—
that you should know who you will be
when the Day of Reckoning arrives.

MATHNAWI III, 2652–54

Burnt Wing

The fowler scatters grain incessantly:
the grain is visible, but the deceit is hidden.
Wherever you see the grain, beware:
a trap may imprison your wings.
The bird that gives up that grain
eats from Reality's spacious field.
It remains contented and free;
no trap seizes its feathers.
Many times have you fallen into the
    snare of greed
and given your throat up to be cut;
but again the One that disposes hearts to
    remorse
has set you free, accepted your repentance,
and made you rejoice.
O moth, don't be forgetful and full of doubt;
just look at your burnt wing.

MATHNAWI III, 2858–61; 2870–71; 2879

Thankfulness, Alertness

Giving thanks for abundance
is sweeter than the abundance itself:
Should one who is absorbed with the
    Generous One
be distracted by the gift?
Thankfulness is the soul of beneficence;
abundance is but the husk,
for thankfulness brings you
to the place where the Beloved lives.
Abundance yields heedlessness;
thankfulness, alertness:
hunt for bounty with the snare of gratitude to
    the King.

MATHNAWI III, 2895–97

A Book Is Not a Pillow

I did not create the Jinn and mankind
*except that they might worship Me.**
Recite this text.
The final object of this world
is nothing but divine worship.
Though the final object of a book
is the knowledge which it contains,
you can also make it a pillow to rest upon;
it will serve as that, too.
But being a pillow was not its real aim.
It was really intended for learning and
    knowledge
and the benefit that comes from these.

MATHNAWI III, 2988–90

*Qur'an: Surah Adh-Dhariyat (The Dust-Scattering
Winds), 51:56.

The Interest without the Capital

The lover's food is the love of the bread;
no bread need be at hand:
no one who is sincere in his love is a slave
   to existence.

Lovers have nothing to do with existence;
lovers have the interest without the capital.

Without wings they fly around the world;
without hands they carry the polo ball
   off the field.

That dervish who caught the scent of Reality
used to weave baskets even though his hand had
   been cut off.

Lovers have pitched their tents in nonexistence:
they are of one quality and one essence, as
   nonexistence is.

MATHNAWI III, 3020–24

Gainful Employment

When it comes to earning food,
why has the fear of eternal disappointment
not waylaid you?
You'll say, "Though I face the fear of
    disappointment,
fear increases when I'm idle.
My hope increases when I work;
when I'm idle, I risk more."
Why does the fear of loss
restrain you when it comes to faith?
Haven't you seen how gainfully employed
the prophets and saints are?
Haven't you seen what mines of treasure
have opened to them
from frequenting the shop of Spirit?

MATHNAWI III, 3096–101

The Reins of Free Will

The power of conscious choice
is your profit earning capital.
Pay attention!
Watch over that moment of power!
The human being rides on the steed of
We have honored the children of Adam.*
The reins of free will are in the hand of
    intelligence.

MATHNAWI III, 3299–3300

*Qur'an: Al-Isra (The Night Journey), 17:70.

Mary's Need

It was Mary's painful need that made
  the infant Jesus
begin to speak from the cradle.
Whatever grew has grown for the sake of those
  in need,
so that a seeker might find the thing he sought.
If God Most High has created the heavens,
He has created them for the purpose of
  satisfying needs.
Wherever a pain is, that's where the cure goes;
wherever poverty is, that's where provision goes.
Wherever a difficult question is,
that's where the answer goes;
wherever a ship is, water goes to it.
Don't seek the water; increase your thirst,
so water may gush forth from above and below.
Until the tender-throated babe is born,
how should the milk for it
flow from the mother's breast?

MATHNAWI III, 3204; 3208–13

Core and Rind

The core of every fruit is better than its rind:
consider the body to be the rind,
and its friend the spirit to be the core.
After all, the Human Being has a goodly core;
seek it for one moment
if you are of those inspired by the
    Divine breath.

MATHNAWI III, 3417–18

Fear of Yourself

Everyone's death is of the same quality
    as himself:
to the enemy of God, an enemy;
to the friend of God, a friend.
Your fear of death in fleeing from it
is really your fear of yourself.
Pay attention, dear soul!

MATHNAWI III, 3439; 3441

God's Deliberation

God manifested the earth and heavenly spheres
through the deliberation of six days—
even though He was able through
    "Be, and it is" *
to bring forth a hundred earths and heavens.
Little by little until forty years of age
that Sovereign raises the human being to
    completion,
although in a single moment He was able
to send fifty flying up from nonexistence.
Jesus by means of one prayer
could make the dead spring to life:
is the Creator of Jesus unable
to suddenly bring full-grown human beings
fold by fold into existence?
This deliberation is for the purpose
    of teaching you
that you must seek God slowly, without any
    break.
A little stream which moves continually

---

*Qur'an: Surah Ya Stu (O Thou Human Being),
36:82.

doesn't become tainted or foul.
From this deliberation are born felicity and joy:
this deliberation is the egg;
good fortune is the bird that comes forth.

MATHNAWI III, 3500–08

Two Wings

Observe the qualities of expansion and
    contraction
in the fingers of your hand:
surely after the closing of the fist comes the
    opening.
If the fingers were always closed or always open,
the owner would be crippled.
Your movement is governed by these two
    qualities:
they are as necessary to you
as two wings are to a bird.

MATHNAWI III, 3762–66

The Beauty

For lovers, the only lecturer
is the beauty of the Beloved:
their only book and lecture and lesson is the
    Face.
Outwardly they are silent,
but their penetrating remembrance rises
to the high throne of their Friend.
Their only lesson
is enthusiasm, whirling, and trembling,
not the precise points of law.

MATHNAWI III, 3847–49

Become More by Dying

O my noble friends, slaughter this cow,
if you wish to raise up the spirit of insight.
I died to being mineral and was transformed.
I died to vegetable growth
and attained to the state of animals.
I died from animality and became Adam:
why then should I fear?
When have I become less by dying?
Next I shall die to being a human being,
so that I may soar and lift up my head among
   the angels.
Yet I must escape even from that angelic
   state:
*everything is perishing except His Face.**
Once again I shall be sacrificed, dying to the
   angelic;
I shall become that which could never be
   imagined —

---

*Qur'an: Surah Al-Qasas (The Story), 28:88.

I shall become nonexistent.
Nonexistence sings its clear melody,
*Truly, unto Him shall we return!**

MATHNAWI III, 3900–06

*Qur'an: Surah Fussilat (Clearly Spelled Out),
41:21.

The Lawsuit

I am amazed at the seeker of purity
who when it's time to be polished
complains of rough handling.
Love is like a lawsuit:
to suffer harsh treatment is the evidence;
when you have no evidence, the lawsuit is lost.
Don't grieve when the Judge demands your
    evidence;
kiss the snake so that you may gain the treasure.
That harshness isn't towards you, O son,
but towards the harmful qualities within you.
When someone beats a rug,
the blows are not against the rug,
but against the dust in it.

MATHNAWI III, 4008–12

The Bloom

That which God said to the rose,
and caused it to laugh in full-blown beauty,
He said to my heart,
and made it a hundred times more beautiful.

MATHNAWI III, 4129

The Godly Art

Everyone baked by the divine Sun
will become rock solid:
without dread or shame,
his features fiery and veil-rending,
like the face of the peerless Sun.
Every prophet was hard-faced in this world,
and beat single-handed against the army of
    kings,
and did not turn his face from fear or pain,
but single and alone
dashed against a whole world.
The stone is hard-faced and bold-eyed,
unafraid of the bricks thrown by the world.
For the bricks were made strong in the kiln,
but the rock was hardened by a Godly art.

MATHNAWI III, 4139–44

Deliverance

Your anguish is seeking a way to attain to Me:
yesterday evening I heard your deep sighs.
And I am able, without any delay,
to give you access, to show you a way of passage,
to deliver you from this whirlpool of time,
that you might set your foot upon
the treasure of union with Me;
but the sweetness and delights of the resting
    place
are in proportion to the pain of the journey.
Only then will you enjoy
your native town and your kinsfolk,
when you have suffered the anguish of exile.

MATHNAWI III, 4154–58

Boil Nicely Now

Look at the chickpeas in the pot,
how they leap up when they feel the fire.
While boiling, one of them rises to the top
and cries, "Why are you setting this fire under
    me?
Did you buy me for this tumbling and torture?"
The housewife keeps hitting it with the ladle.
"No!" she says, "boil nicely now,
and don't leap away from the one who makes
    the fire.
It's not because you are hateful to me that I boil
    you,
but so that you might gain flavor,
and become nutritious and mingle with
    essential spirit.
This affliction is not because you are despised.
When you were green and fresh,
you were watered in the garden:
that watering was for the sake of this fire."

MATHNAWI III, 4159–65

The River

Time is limited; the abundant water is flowing
    away.
Drink, before you fall to pieces.
There is a famous conduit, full of the
    Water of Life:
draw the Water, so that you may become
    fruitful.
We are drinking the water of Khidr*
from the river of the speech of the saints:
Come, thirsty one!
Even if you don't see the water,
as skillfully as a blind person,
bring the jug to the river and dip it in.

MATHNAWI III, 4300–04

---

*Khidr is the immortal "Green Man" who appears
as a guide to those who are worthy.

The Water Is Calling the Thirsty

Surely there is a window from heart to heart:
they are not separate and far from each other.
Though two earthenware lamps are not joined,
their light mingles.
No lover seeks union without the beloved
    seeking;
but the love of lovers
makes the body thin as a bowstring,
while the love of loved ones
makes them shapely and pleasing.
When the lightning of love for the beloved
has shot into this heart,
know that there is love in that heart.
When love for God has been doubled in
    your heart,
there is no doubt that God has love for you.
No sound of clapping comes forth from only
    one hand.
The thirsty man is moaning,
"O delicious water!"

The water is calling,
"Where is the one who will drink me?"
This thirst in our souls is the magnetism of the
    Water:
We are Its, and It is ours.

MATHNAWI III, 4390–99

In Mutual Embrace

The desire in the female for the male
is so that they may perfect each other's work.
God put desire in man and woman
in order that the world
should be preserved by this union.
God instills the desire of every part for the
    other:
from their union, creation results.
And so night and day are in mutual embrace:
they appear to be opposites, even enemies,
but the truth they serve is one,
each desiring the other like kin,
for the perfection of their work.
Both serve one purpose, for without night,
human nature would receive no income:
what then could day expend?

MATHNAWI III, 4414–20

Lovers Are Made Aware

You make a hundred resolutions
to journey somewhere,
but He draws you somewhere else.
He turns the horse's bridle in every direction
so that the untrained horse may know there
    is a rider.
The clever horse is well paced
because it knows a rider is mounted upon it.
He fixed your heart on a hundred passionate
    desires,
disappointed you, and then broke your heart.
Since He broke the wings of your first intention,
how do you doubt the existence of the
    Wing-breaker?
Since His ordainment snapped the cord
of your contrivance,
how can you remain blind to His Command?
Your resolutions and aims now and then are
    fulfilled
so that through hope your heart
might form another intention
which He might once again destroy.

For if He were to keep you completely from
    success,
you would despair:
how would the seed of expectation be sown?
If your heart did not sow that seed,
and then encounter barrenness,
how would it recognize its submission to Divine
    will?
By their failures lovers are made aware of their
    Lord.
Lack of success is the guide to Paradise:
Pay attention to the tradition,
"Paradise is encompassed with pain."*

MATHNAWI III, 4456–67

Hadith, a saying of the Prophet Muhammad.

The Shadow Loves the Sun

The lover hotly pursues the beloved:
when the beloved comes, the lover is gone.
You are a lover of God, and God is such
that when He comes not a single hair of yours
    remains.
At that look of His a hundred like you vanish
    away.
I think you are in love with nothingness.
You are a shadow and in love with the sun.
When the sun comes, the shadow quickly
    disappears.

MATHNAWI III, 4620–23

Consider

Because of a fractured leg,
God bestows a wing;
likewise from the depths of the pit,
He opens a door of escape.
God said, "Don't consider
whether you're up a tree or in a hole:
consider Me, for I am the Key of the Way."*

MATHNAWI III, 4808–09

Hadith Qudsi, an extra-Qur'anic revelation.

O Drop

Listen, O drop, give yourself up without regret,
and in exchange gain the Ocean.
Listen, O drop, bestow upon yourself this
    honor,
and in the arms of the Sea be secure.
Who indeed should be so fortunate?
An Ocean wooing a drop!
In God's name, in God's name, sell and buy at
    once!
Give a drop, and take this Sea full of pearls.

MATHNAWI IV, 2619–22

Ask the Rose about the Rose

The interpretation of a sacred text is true
if it stirs you to hope, activity, and awe;
and if it makes you slacken your service,
know the real truth to be this:
it's a distortion of the sense of the saying,
not a true interpretation.
This saying has come down
to inspire you to serve—
that God may take the hands
of those who have lost hope.
Ask the meaning of the Qur'an from
   the Qur'an alone,
and from that one who has set fire
to his idle fancy and burned it away,
and has become a sacrifice to the Qur'an,
bowing low in humbleness,
so that the Qur'an has become the essence of
   his spirit.
The essential oil that has utterly devoted itself
   to the rose,
you can smell either that oil or the rose, as you
   please.

MATHNAWI V, 3125–30

Heroes

Does any artist paint for the sake of the picture
    itself,
without the hope of offering some good?
No, but for the sake of the viewers and the
    young
who will be drawn by it and freed from cares.
Or does any potter hastily throw a pot or a bowl
without any thought of what it will hold?
Does any calligrapher write for the script alone
without any regard for the reader?

The external form is for the sake of
    something unseen,
and that took shape for something else unseen.
Just as the moves in a game of chess
reveal the results of each move in what follows.
They make one move to conceal another move,
and that for something else, and so on and on.
So move on, aware of reasons within reasons,
one move after another, to checkmate.

One step is for the sake of another,
like the rungs of a ladder, to reach the roof.

The hunger for food produces semen;
semen is for procreation,
and the light in the parents' eyes.

Someone with dulled vision sees no further
than this:
his intelligence has no movement; it vegetates.
Whether a plant is summoned or not,
it stays planted within the soil.
Don't be deceived if the wind bends it.
Its head says: "We obey the zephyr's request,"
while its feet say, "Leave us alone!"
Since he does not know how to move,
he advances on trust like the blind.
Consider what acting on trust means in a war:
it's like a gambler trusting the throw of the
dice.

But if someone's insight is unfrozen,
it penetrates the veil.
He sees with his own eye in the present
what will come to pass in ten years time.
In the same way, every one perceives
the invisible future, whether good or bad,
according to the measure of his insight.

When the barriers in front and behind are
    removed,
the eye penetrates and reads the Tablet of the
    Unseen.
When he looks back to the origin of existence,
the beginning and all the past display
    themselves,
including the argument between the angels
    of earth
and the Divine Majesty, their resistance
to recognizing our Father Adam as
    God's steward.

And when he casts his eye forward,
he sees all that will come to pass until
    the Gathering.
Therefore he sees back to the root of the root,
and forward to the Day of Decision.
Anyone, to the degree of his enlightenment,
sees as much as he has polished of himself.
The more he polishes, the more he sees,
the more visible do the forms become.
If you say purity is by the grace of God,
this success in polishing is also through that
    Generosity.

That work and prayer is in proportion to the
    yearning:
*People have nothing but what they
    have striven for.*

God alone is the giver of aspiration:
no rough brute aspires to kingliness,
nor does God's gift of good fortune preclude
one's own consent and will and choice.
But when He brings trouble upon some
    ill-fated person,
he ungratefully packs off in flight.
Whereas when God brings trouble upon a
    blessed man,
he just draws nearer to God.
In battle the cowardly, from fear of their lives,
have chosen their means of escape.
But heroes are borne forward by their fear and
    pain.
From fear, too, the weak soul dies within itself.
Tribulation and fear for one's life are
    touchstones
to distinguish the cowardly from the brave.

Kabir Helminski
MATHNAWI IV, 2881FF

Buttermilk

These creatures of the world exist
to manifest the divine treasure.
God said, "I was a hidden treasure."
Listen, don't let your substance be wasted.
Become manifest!
Your true sincerity is hidden in falsehood,
like the taste of butter in buttermilk.
For years this buttermilk, which is the body,
is obvious and manifest, while the butter,
which is spirit, has disappeared within it.
Until Truth sends a messenger, a servant,
a shaker of the buttermilk in the churn,
who has the skill and the method for churning,
so that I may discover that my true self was
    hidden.
Or until the words of a servant of that
    messenger
enter the ear of one who is seeking inspiration.
The ear of the faithful retains the inspiration,
because such an ear is close to the caller,
just as an infant's ear is filled with its mother's
    words
until it learns to speak.

And if the infant's ear is not right,
it fails to hear its mother's words and is mute.
Anyone born deaf remains mute.
Only one who hears the mother's words learns
    to speak.
Know that this deafness is a defect,
for the deaf ear does not hear the words
and so cannot learn.
Only God, whose attributes are perfect,
possessed speech without being taught.
And Adam whom God taught without
a mother or nurse between,
or the Messiah who was taught by Love
and came into the world with the Word,
so that he could defend himself
from accusations of an illegitimate birth.
A lot of shaking is needed
for the buttermilk to offer up the butter from its
    heart.
The butter is as invisible as nonexistence itself,
while the buttermilk has raised its own banner
    in the world.
What seems most to exist is just the skin
of something which seems not to exist but is the
    source.

If the buttermilk has not yet offered its butter,
store it away until you can extract the butter.
Churn it from side to side, hand to hand,
until it reveals what is hidden within it.
For this perishable body is the evidence of the
    eternal,
and the babbling of the drunkard
is proof that someone poured the wine.

MATHNAWI IV, 3030

The Water We Seek

The eye or the spirit that focuses on the
    transient
falls on its face wherever it goes.
Someone who focuses on the distance,
without knowledge, may see far,
but just as we do in a dream.

Asleep on the bank of a river, lips parched,
you dream you are running towards water.
In the distance you see the water of your desire
and, caught by your seeing, you run towards it.

In the dream you boast,
"I am the one whose heart can see through
    the veils."
Yet every step carries you further away
toward the perilous mirage.
From the moment you dreamed you set out
you created the distance
from that which had been near to you.
Many set out on a journey
that leads them further away from their goal.

The intuitive claims of the sleeper are a fantasy.
You, too, are sleepy; but for God's sake,
if you must sleep, sleep on the Way of God,
and maybe some other seeker on the Way
will awaken you from your fantasies and
    slumber.

No matter how subtle the sleeper's thought
    becomes,
his dreams will not guide him Home.
Whether the sleeper's thought is twofold or
    threefold,
it is error multiplying error.

While he dreams of running through the
    wilderness,
the waves are lapping so near.
While he dreams of the pangs of thirst,
the water is *nearer than his jugular vein.*

Kabir Helminski
MATHNAWI IV, 3226–41

Whispers of Love

Love whispers in my ear,
"Better to be a prey than a hunter.
Make yourself My fool.
Stop trying to be the sun and become a speck!
Dwell at My door and be homeless.
Don't pretend to be a candle, be a moth,
so you may taste the savor of Life
and know the power hidden in serving."

MATHNAWI V, 411–14

The Six-Faced Mirror

The Prophet said, "God doesn't pay attention to
   your outer form:
so in your improvising, seek the owner of the
   Heart."
God says, "I regard you through the owner of
   the Heart,
not because of prostrations in prayer
nor the giving of wealth in charity."*
The owner of the Heart becomes a six-faced
   mirror:
through him God looks out upon all the six
   directions.

MATHNAWI V, 869–70; 874

*Hadith Qudsi, an extra-Qur'anic revelation.

Only the Heart

If a wealthy person brings a hundred sacks
 of gold,
God will only say,
"Bring the Heart, you who are bent double.
If the Heart is pleased with you, I am pleased;
and if the Heart is opposed to you, I am
 opposed.
I don't pay attention to 'you'; I look to the heart:
bring it, poor soul, as a gift to My door!
Its relation to you is also mine:
Paradise is at the feet of mothers."*
The heart is the mother and father
and origin of all creatures:
the one who knows the heart from the skin
 is blessed.
You will say, "Look, I have brought a heart
 to You."
God will respond, "The world is full of
 these hearts.

Hadith, a saying of the Prophet Muhammad.

Bring the heart that is the axis of the world
and the soul of the soul of the soul of Adam."
The Ruler of all hearts is waiting
for a heart filled with light and goodness.

MATHNAWI V, 881–88

Why Are You Milking Another?

Strip the raiment of pride from your body:
in learning, put on the garment of humility.
Soul receives from soul the knowledge of
    humility,
not from books or speech.
Though mysteries of spiritual poverty
are within the seeker's heart,
she doesn't yet possess knowledge of those
    mysteries.
Let her wait until her heart expands and fills
    with Light:
God said, "*Did We not expand your breast . . . ?**
For We have put illumination there,
We have put the expansion into your heart."
When you are a source of milk,
why are you milking another?
An endless fountain of milk is within you:
why are you seeking milk with a pail?
You are a lake with a channel to the Sea:
be ashamed to seek water from a pool;

---

*Qur'an: Surah Ash-Sharh (The Opening of the
Heart), 94:1.

for *did We not expand your chest* . . . ?
Again, don't you possess the expansion?
Why are you going about like a beggar?
Contemplate the expansion of the heart
    within you,
that you may not be reproached with,
    Do you not see?*

MATHNAWI V, 1061; 1064–72

*Qur'an: Surah Adh-Dhariyat (The Dust-Scattering
Winds) 51:21.

Borrowed Clothes

That servant for whom the world lovingly wept
the world now rejects: what did he do wrong?
His crime was that he put on borrowed clothes
and pretended he owned them.
We take them back, in order that he may know
    for sure
that the stock is Ours
and the well dressed are only borrowers;
that he may know that those robes were a loan,
a ray from the Sun of Being.
All that beauty, power, virtue, and excellence
have arrived here from the Sun of Excellence.
They, the light of that Sun, turn back again,
like the stars, from these bodily walls.
When the Sunbeam has returned home,
every wall is left darkened and black.
That which amazed you in the faces of the fair
is the Light of the Sun
reflected in the three-colored glass.
The glasses of diverse hue
cause the Light to assume color for us.
When the many-colored glasses are no longer,
then the colorless Light amazes you.

Make it your habit to behold
the Light without the glass,
so that when the glass is shattered
you may not be left blind.

MATHNAWI V, 981–91

The Good Root

Are you fleeing from Love because of a single
    humiliation?
What do you know of Love except the name?
Love has a hundred forms of pride and disdain,
and is gained by a hundred means of
    persuasion.
Since Love is loyal, it purchases one who is
    loyal:
it has no interest in a disloyal companion.
The human being resembles a tree;
your root is a covenant with God:
that root must be cherished with all one's might.
A feeble covenant is a rotten root, without grace
    or fruit.
Though the boughs and leaves of the date palm
    are green,
greenness brings no benefit if the root is
    corrupt.
If a branch is without green leaves, yet has a
    good root,
a hundred leaves will put forth their hands in
    the end.

MATHNAWI V, 1163–69

The Ruby

At breakfast tea a beloved asked her lover,
"Who do you love more, yourself or me?"

"From my head to my foot I have become you.
Nothing remains of me but my name.
You have your wish. Only you exist.
I've disappeared like a drop of vinegar
in an ocean of honey."

A stone which has become a ruby
is filled with the qualities of the sun.
No stoniness remains in it.
If it loves itself, it is loving the sun.
And if it loves the sun, it is loving itself.
There is no difference between these two loves.

Before the stone becomes the ruby, it is its own
    enemy.
Not one but two exist.
The stone is dark and blind to daylight.
If it loves itself, it is unfaithful: it intensely resists
    the sun.
If it says "I," it is all darkness.
A pharaoh claims divinity and is brought down.

Hallaj says the same and is saved.
One I is cursed, another I is blessed.
One I is a stone, another a crystal.
One an enemy of the light, the other a reflector
   of it.
In its inmost consciousness, not through any
   doctrine,
it is one with the light.

Work on your stony qualities
and become resplendent like the ruby.
Practice self-denial and accept difficulty.
Always see infinite life in letting the self die.
Your stoniness will decrease;
your ruby nature will grow.
The signs of self-existence will leave your body,
and ecstasy will take you over.

Become all hearing like an ear and gain a ruby
   earring.
Dig a well in the earth of this body,
or even before the well is dug,
let God draw the water up.

Be always at work scraping the dirt from the
  well.
To everyone who suffers,
perseverance brings good fortune.
The Prophet has said that each prostration of
  prayer
is a knock on heaven's door.
When anyone continues to knock,
felicity shows its smiling face.

Kabir Helminski
MATHNAWI V, 2020FF

Livelihood

Trust in God is the best livelihood.
Everyone needs to trust in God
and ask, "O God, bring this work of mine
   to success."
Prayer involves trust in God, and trust in God
is the only means of livelihood
that is independent of all others.
In these two worlds I don't know
of any means of livelihood
better than trust in our Sustainer.
I know nothing better than gratitude
which brings in its wake the daily bread and its
   increase.

MATHNAWI V, 2425–26

Your Bread Is Seeking You

Listen, put trust in God,
don't let your hands and feet tremble with fear:
your daily bread is more in love with you,
than you with it.

It is in love with you and is holding back
only because it knows of your lack of self-denial.

If you had any self-denial, the daily bread
would throw itself upon you as lovers do.
What is this feverish trembling for fear of
  hunger?
With trust in God one can live full-fed.

MATHNAWI V, 2851–54

The Froth and the Sea

The one who regards the foam explains the
    mystery,
while the one who regards the Sea is
    bewildered.
The one who regards the foam forms intentions,
while the one who has known the Sea
makes her heart one with the Sea.
The one who regards the froth calculates and
    reckons,
while the one who regards the Sea
is without conscious volition.
The one who regards the froth is continually in
    motion,
while the one who regards the Sea is free of
    hypocrisy.

MATHNAWI V, 2908–11

Love Ends All Arguments

Dear soul, Love alone cuts arguments short,
for it alone comes to the rescue
when you cry for help against disputes.
Eloquence is dumbfounded by Love:
it dares not wrangle,
for the lover fears that, if he answers back,
the pearl of inner experience
might fall out of his mouth.

MATHNAWI V, 3240–41

The Guest House

Darling, the body is a guest house;
every morning someone new arrives.
Don't say, "O, another weight around
  my neck!"
or your guest will fly back to nothingness.
Whatever enters your heart is a guest
from the invisible world: entertain it well.

Every day and every moment a thought comes
like an honored guest into your heart.
My soul, regard each thought as a person,
for every person's true value
is in the quality of thought they hold.

If a sorrowful thought stands in the way,
it is also preparing the way for joy.
It furiously sweeps your house clean,
in order that some new joy
may appear from the Source.
It scatters the withered leaves
from the bough of the heart,
in order that fresh green leaves might grow.
It uproots the old joy so that
a new joy may enter from Beyond.

Sorrow pulls up the rotten root
that was hidden from sight.
Whatever sorrow takes away
or causes the heart to sacrifice,
it puts something better in its place—
especially for one who is certain
that sorrow is the servant of the intuitive.

Without the frown of clouds and lightning,
the vines would be burned by the smiling sun.
Both good and bad luck
become guests in your heart:
like planets traveling from sign to sign.
When something transits your sign,
adapt yourself,
and be as harmonious as its ruling sign,
so that when it rejoins the Moon,
it will speak kindly to the Lord of the heart.

Whenever sorrows comes again,
meet it with smiles and laughter,
saying, "O my Creator, save me from its harm:
and do not deprive me of its good.
Lord, remind me to be thankful,
let me feel no regret if its benefit passes away.

"And if the pearl is not in sorrow's hand,
let it go and still be pleased.
Increase your sweet practice.
Your practice will benefit you at another time;
someday your need will be suddenly fulfilled."

Kabir Helminski
MATHNAWI V, 3644–46; 3676–88; 3693–96;
3700–01

The One-Way Pull

O my Sustainer.
deliver me from this imprisonment of freewill.
The one-way pull on *the straight Path**
is better than the two-way pull of perplexity.
Though You are the only goal of these two ways,
still this duality is agonizing to the spirit.

Though the destination of these two ways is You
    alone,
still the battle is never like the banquet.
Listen to the explanation God gave in the
    Qur'an:
they shrank from bearing it.†
This perplexity in the heart is like war:
when a man is perplexed he says,
"I wonder whether this is better for my situation
    or that."

*Qur'an: Surah Al-Fatihah (The Opening), 1:6.
†Qur'an: Surah Al-Azhab (The Confederates),
33:72.

In perplexity the fear of failure and the hope of
   success
always are in conflict with each other,
advancing, retreating.
From You came this ebb and flow within me;
otherwise this sea of mine would be still.
From that source from which You gave me this
   perplexity,
likewise now, graciously give me clarity.

MATHNAWI VI, 203–11

Consult Your Own Hearts

To follow one's own desires is to flee from God
and to spill the blood of spirituality
in the presence of His justice.

This world is a trap, and desire is its bait:
escape the traps, and quickly
turn your face towards God.

When you have followed this Way,
you have enjoyed a hundred blessings.
When you have gone the opposite way,
you have fared ill.

So the Prophet said, "Consult your own hearts,
even though the religious judge
advises you about worldly affairs."

Abandon desire, and so reveal His Mercy:
you've learned by experience
the sacrifice He requires.

Since you can't escape, be His servant,
and go from His prison into His rose garden.
When you continually keep watch
over your thoughts and actions,

you are always seeing the Justice and the Judge;
though heedlessness may shut your eyes,
still, that doesn't stop the sun from shining.

MATHNAWI VI, 377–84

The Sound of Water in the Ears of the Thirsty

The real work belongs to someone who desires
    God
and has severed himself from every other work.

The rest are like children who play together
for these few short days until it gets dark.
Or like someone who awakes
and springs up, still drowsy,
and then is lulled back to sleep
by the suggestion of an evil nurse:
"Go to sleep, my darling,
I won't let anyone disturb you."

If you are wise, you, yourself,
will tear up your slumber by the roots,
like the thirsty man who heard the noise
    of the water.

God says to you, "I am the sound of water
in the ears of the thirsty;
I am rain falling from heaven.
Spring up, lover, show some excitement!
How can you hear the sound of water
and then fall back asleep!"

MATHNAWI VI, 586–92

The Ship Sunk in Love

Should Love's heart rejoice unless I burn?
For my heart is Love's dwelling.
If You will burn Your house, burn it, Love!
Who will say, "It's not allowed"?
Burn this house thoroughly!
The lover's house improves with fire.
From now on I will make burning my aim,
for I am like the candle:
burning only makes me brighter.
Abandon sleep tonight; traverse for one night
the region of the sleepless.
Look upon these lovers who have become
    distraught
and like moths have died
in union with the One Beloved.
Look upon this ship of God's creatures
and see how it is sunk in Love.

MATHNAWI VI, 617–23

Everyone Is Dying

Everyone in the world, whether man or
    woman,
is dying and continually passing through the
    agony of death.
Regard their words as the final injunctions
which a father gives his son. In this way
consideration and compassion may grow in
    your heart,
and the root of hatred and jealousy may be cut
    away.
Look upon your kinsman with that intention,
that your heart may burn with pity for his death
    agony.
Everything that is coming will come:
consider it to have already arrived;
consider your friend to be already
in the throes of death, losing his life.
If selfish motives prevent you from this
    insight,
cast them from your heart;
and if you cannot cast them out,
don't stand inertly in incapacity:
know that with every one who feels incapable,

there is a goodly Incapacitator.
Incapacity is a chain laid upon you:
you must open your eye to behold
the One who lays the chain.

MATHNAWI VI, 761–68

The Sea within the Fish

A human being is essentially an eye;
the rest is merely flesh and skin:
whatever the eye has beheld, he is that.
A jar will submerge a mountain with its water
when the eye of the jar is open to the Sea.
When the interior of the jar has a channel to
   the Sea,
that jar will overwhelm a river as great as the
   Oxus.
In the same way whatever speech Muhammad
   utters,
those words are really uttered by the Sea.
All his words were pearls of the Sea,
for his heart had a passage into that Sea.
Since the bounty of the Sea is poured through
   our jar,
why should anyone be amazed that the Sea
   itself
should be contained in a Fish*?

MATHNAWI VI, 812–17

*The Perfect Human Being.

The Best Customer

If you want a customer who will pay in gold,
could there be a better customer than God,
O my heart? He buys our dirty bag of goods,
and in return gives us an inner light
lent from His splendor.
He receives the dissolving ice of this mortal
    body
and gives a kingdom beyond imagining.
He takes a few teardrops,
and gives a spiritual spring so delicious
sugar is jealous of its sweetness.
If any doubt waylays you,
rely upon the spiritual traders, the prophets.
The Divine Ruler increased their fortune so
    greatly,
no mountain could bear what they've been
    given.

MATHNAWI VI, 879–82; 886–87

You Are an Eye

Since you have perceived the dust of forms,
perceive the wind that moves them;
since you have perceived the foam,
perceive the ocean of Creative Energy.

Come, perceive it, for in you
insight is all that matters;
the rest is just fat and flesh,
a weft and warp of bones and muscle.

Your fat never increased the light in candles;
your flesh never became roast-meat
for someone drunk with spiritual wine.
Dissolve this whole body of yours in vision:

pass into sight, pass into sight, pass into sight!
One sight perceives only two yards ahead;
another sight has beheld the two worlds
and the Face of the King.

Between these two
is an incalculable difference:
seek the remedy of vision,
and God best knows that which is hidden.

MATHNAWI VI, 1460–65

Love Is Reckless

Love is reckless; not reason.
Reason seeks a profit.
Love comes on strong, consuming herself,
     unabashed.

Yet, in the midst of suffering,
Love proceeds like a millstone,
hard-surfaced and straightforward.

Having died to self-interest,
she risks everything and asks for nothing.
Love gambles away every gift God bestows.

Without cause God gave us Being;
without cause, give it back again.
Gambling yourself away is beyond any religion.

Religion seeks grace and favor,
but those who gamble these away
     are God's favorites,
for they neither put God to the test
nor knock at the door of gain and loss.

Kabir Helminski
MATHNAWI VI, 1967–74

Out of Control

If I had any judgment and skill of my own,
my consideration and plans
would all be under my control.

At night my consciousness
would not leave against my will,
and the birds of my senses
would be secured within my own cage.

I would be aware of the stages journeyed
    by the soul
in unconsciousness, in sleep, and in times of
    trouble.

But since my hand is made empty
by His sovereign power to loosen and to bind,

O, I wonder,
from whom comes this self-conceit of mine?

MATHNAWI VI, 2324–27

Why Be Cruel to Yourself

Your grace is the shepherd of all
who have been created,
guarding them from the wolf of pain—
a loving shepherd like God's pen, Moses.
A single sheep fled from him: Moses wore out
   his shoes
and his feet blistered as he followed after it.
He continued searching until night fell;
meanwhile the flock had vanished from sight.
The lost sheep was weak and exhausted;
Moses shook the dust from it
and stroked its back and head with his hand,
fondling it lovingly like a mother.
Not a bit of irritation and anger,
nothing but love and pity and tears!
He said to the sheep, "I can understand
that you naturally had no pity on me,
but why did your nature show such cruelty
   to itself?"
At that moment God said to the angels,
"This human being is suitable to be a prophet."

MATHNAWI VI, 3280–87

Generosity Is Gainful Trade

O sea of bliss, You have stored
transcendental forms of consciousness in the
    heedless,
You have stored a wakefulness in sleep,
You have fastened dominion over the heart
to the state of one who has lost her heart.

You conceal riches in the lowliness of poverty,
You fasten the necklace of wealth
to poverty's iron collar.
Opposite is secretly concealed in opposite:
fire is hidden within boiling water.
A delightful garden is hidden within Nimrod's
    fire.

Income multiplies from giving and spending—
so that Muhammad, the king of prosperity, has
    said,
"O possessors of wealth, generosity is a gainful
    trade."
Riches were never lessened by sharing:
in truth, acts of charity increase one's wealth.

MATHNAWI VI, 3567–73

Losing the Way

What wisdom was this,
that the Object of all desire
caused me to leave my home joyously
on a fool's errand,
so that I was actually rushing to lose the way
and at each moment being taken
farther from what I sought—
and then God in His beneficence
made that very wandering
the means of my reaching the right road
and finding wealth!

He makes losing the way a way to true faith;
He makes going astray a field
for the harvest of righteousness,
so that no righteous one may be without fear
and no traitor may be without hope.
The Gracious One has put the antidote in the
    poison
so that they may say He is the Lord of hidden
    grace.

MATHNAWI VI, 4339–44

Animal Cookies

God gives the things of this earth
a certain color and variety and value,
causing childish folk to argue over it.

When a piece of dough is baked
in the shape of a camel or lion,
these children bite their fingers excitedly in
    their greed.

Both lion and camel turn to bread in the
    mouth,
but it's futile to tell this to children.

MATHNAWI VI, 4717–19

The Tale of the Bedouin and His Wife

One night a Bedouin woman said to her husband: "We are suffering hardship and poverty, while all the world is better off than us, and we alone are unhappy. We have no bread and our only condiment is envy. We have no jug and our only water is our tears. Our only clothing by day is the burning sunshine, and at night only the moonbeams cover us. We imagine the moon to be a loaf of pita bread and we stretch our hands toward the sky. The poorest of the poor are embarrassed before our poverty . . . What gifts can we give? We are such beggars we would slit the vein of a gnat in the air. If any guest ever arrived here, I swear I would go for his tattered coat in the middle of the night."

Her husband answered her: "How long will you seek money and seed to sow? What is left of our lives? Most of it is past. A sensible person doesn't dwell on getting more or having less, because both will pass like a torrent, and whether the torrent is limpid and clear or just a turbid flood, don't speak of it for it passes in a moment . . .

"The dove on the tree is singing praises even though its evening meal is not yet prepared. The falcon has made the King's pleasure his joy and is disinterested in carrion. Every animal, from the gnat to the elephant, knows it is part of God's family and what nourishment does God provide!

"All of the worries that arise within our breast arise from the dust and wind of our existence. Sorrow uproots like a scythe, and every pain is a piece of death. Expel this death if you can, and if you cannot escape a part of death, know that eventually the whole of it will be poured upon your head. But if that part of death has become sweet to you, know that God will make the whole of it sweet.

"Whoever lives sweetly dies bitterly; whoever serves only the body loses the soul. Sheep are herded from the fields to the town. The fatter they are, the faster they are killed. Night is gone and dawn has come. How long will you tell the same old tale of gold. You were young and contented once. Now you want gold. Once you yourself were the gold.

"You are my wife. Husband and wife must be equals for things to go well. If a pair of shoes must match each other, marriage partners must also match each other. If one of the shoes is tight, the pair is of no use. Have you ever seen a pair of folding doors of unequal size? Or a wolf mated to a lion of the jungle? Or one camel's bag much heavier than the other?

"I am going toward contentment with a strong heart, while you are complaining more and more."

Then the wife answered: "You hypocrite. Reputation is your religion. I am not under your spell anymore. I've had enough of your pretension and nonsense. Your pompous words are unfortunately accompanied by your actions. If you could see yourself you'd be ashamed. When did you ever know real contentment, except for the word? The Prophet said, 'Contentment is a treasure,' but you have confused the pain with the gain. Contentment is the soul's treasure. Don't boast of possessing it, O pain of my soul. Don't call yourself my husband. Don't display your fraudulent affection. My partner is justice not fraudulence. Don't look at me with your cold contempt, or I'll tell everyone what flows in your veins. You think you're so superior. Have you really known what is inside of me?

"You have tried to beguile me with the Name of God. But if I was beguiled by God's Name, you certainly deserve no credit for it. You tried to make the Name of God your trap. Don't be surprised if that Name takes its vengeance on you for my sake. I surrender my body and soul to the name of God." And so she continued to recite volumes of this kind of abuse.

"O woman," he said, "Are you a woman or the father of sorrow? Poverty is my pride, but poverty is beyond your comprehension. Because dervishes are beyond property and wealth, they possess an abundant portion from the Almighty. God the Most High is just. How could He be tyrannical toward the poor and weak? I desire nothing from created beings.

Through contentment I have found a world within my heart. But you, as if sitting on the high branch of a pear tree, see things in your own distorted way. Why don't you come down to the ground where you may lose your strange way of thinking? If someone spins round and round, it looks as if the whole world is spinning, but really you are the one who is revolving."

When the wife saw how fierce her husband had become, she began to weep. Tears are a woman's lure. "I never imagined you would talk to me like this. I hoped for something else from you." She adopted the strategy of deference. "I am your dust, an unworthy wife. My soul and my body, everything I am is yours. If poverty has driven me to desperation, it is not for my own sake, but for yours. You have always been the remedy for my afflictions. I am unwilling to see you penniless. By my soul and conscience, this was not for my sake, but all my sorrow was for your sake. By God, I would die for you. Since I have earned your displeasure, my own body and soul tire me. Gold and silver are less than dirt to me now.

You are the only comfort of my soul. Remember when I was as beautiful as an idol, and you were the idol worshipper? I, your slave, have kindled my heart to comply with you . . . I am your spinach, so cook me any way you wish. My blasphemy has turned to faith. Let your own conscience plead on my behalf. I leave the outcome to your own noble nature."
While she spoke these words through her own tears—she who was a charmer even without tears—lightning flashed in the midst of this downpour, a spark of fire that entered the lonely man's heart. What hope is there when a woman whose beauty is enough to enslave a man becomes herself his slave? A woman whose haughtiness could cause a man to tremble falls weeping at his feet. God has arranged that the beauty of woman *is decked out for man*. How can a man escape from what God has arranged? Inasmuch as He created woman as a comfort to man, how can Adam escape from Eve? If outwardly a man seems to dominate his wife, inwardly he is dominated and is seeking her love. This is a human characteristic; animals do not possess this love.

The Prophet said that Woman prevails over the wise man, while, on the other hand, the ignorant man prevails over her.

And so he began to feel sorry for her and all the things that he had said. He began to wonder how he could have ever been critical of her who was the life of his soul. The man said, "My dear wife, I am sorry. I have been faithless, but now I am surrendered. If I have sinned against you, don't dig me up by my roots."

And so, if you are seeking some moral from the story of the argument between the Bedouin and his wife, consider it an analogy of your own flesh and reason. The man and the wife are both necessary for the manifestation of good and evil. This couple is engaged day and night in this argument in this house of earth. The wife is craving things for the household: bread and other morsels, good name and the approval of society. Like the wife, your flesh has recourse sometimes to humility and sometimes domination. Reason, however, is unaware of all these desires and in its brain is nothing but the love of God. Now listen to this tale in its entirety. If a spiritual explanation were enough, the creation of this whole world would have been an idle undertaking.

If love consisted only of spiritual meaning, the forms of fasting and prayer would not be necessary. The gifts that lovers give to each other are, compared to love itself, nothing but forms. And yet these gifts are testimony to the secret of love. May we be given the discernment to know the false indication from the true.

The man said, "I won't oppose you any longer. Whatever you ask me to do, I will do. I dissolve my existence in yours, because I am your lover. Love makes me blind and deaf."

The wife said, "I wonder if your words are true, or whether you are trying to seduce me and learn my secret."

"No, by God," he said, "Who knows what is most hidden and Who created Adam pure and placed in him all that the tablets of destiny and the world of spirits contain. When the angels saw and heard Adam and his knowledge of the divine names, they said, "Before this time, we had a friendship with the dust of the earth and were planting the seeds of sacredness. We often asked ourselves, why do we who are pure light have this friendship with darkness? Adam, that friendship was in expectation of the scent of you, because that dust formed the warp and woof of your body. When God first asked us to come here, it was a bitter request, and we argued: will you sell the splendor of our praise for this earthly banter and nonsense? But God's decree was an invitation to be bold. He said, 'Isn't My Mercy so much greater than my wrath?' In order to make the superiority of my Mercy even clearer I have to allow this perplexity and doubt. I must allow you to speak and not take offense at what is said. Within this Mercy a hundred mothers and fathers appear and vanish. The mercies of all these parents are only the foam on the sea of My mercy. Their mercy comes and goes, while Mine remains forever. By the truth of that foam and that pure sea, I swear that my words are not meant to test you. My words are from sincerity and humbleness. If you think my words might not be true, put me to the test. Reveal you secret desire, so I may show you my inner secret. Ask me to do anything, so that I may accept whatever I am capable of doing."

"The sun has begun to shine," said the wife, "in the form of a great Caliph in Baghdad. If you can gain access to that King, you yourself will become a king. Otherwise you will only continue to dwell amidst misfortune. Companionship with the fortunate is like an elixir."

"How shall I approach this Caliph? What pretext may I present?"

God has said, "Come, ye," in order to dispel our feelings of shame.

"What can I show to him that will make my own lack of means clear? Because the Caliph requires truth, not pretension."

"When anyone stands up, purified of self-existence, that is the unpretentious truth. Take this jug of rainwater as a gift and depart for the presence of the Caliph. Tell him, 'There is no more precious gift in the desert than this. Even if his treasury is full of gold and jewels, he doesn't get water like this.'"

What is this jug if not this limiting body of ours, filled with the briny water of our senses.

We have been told, "God has bought the be-
lievers lives in return for paradise." It's a jug
with five spouts; keep it pure, so that you can
carry it to the King, and the King will pur-
chase it from you. Close your eyes to vain desire. Stop up its spouts, and keep it filled with
water from the Sea of Reality.

"Yes, I am sure the Caliph has never received a gift like this before. Stop up the
mouth of the jug, and sew a felt covering for
it, so that it may arrive safely to the Caliph and
he may use it to break his fast. There is no
water like this in the world." How could he
know what the Caliph's circumstances might
be, since he had never escaped his own fleet-
ing caravansary? His hands trembled all the
way to Baghdad as he carried his precious gift.

Meanwhile, his wife unrolled the prayer
carpet and prayed to her Lord for the water's
safe journey to the Sea! "My husband is quite
clever," she thought, "but our treasure will
face many enemies."

When he did finally arrive in Baghdad he
saw before him a bountiful court with many
who were seeking help. High and low, they

were all quickened with life, like the whole world arising to the trumpet of the Resurrection. He heard a loud call: "Come, seekers. Abundance is seeking beggars, just as beauty seeks a mirror." Beggars are the mirrors of God's abundance, and those who have united with God become that abundance.

The court officers of the Caliph were at the Palace sprinkling rose water on all comers. It was their duty to assess the need of each and fulfill it even before being asked. "O chief of the Arabs, how has your journey been?"

"I am a stranger," he said, "and I have come from the desert in hope of gaining the grace of the Sultan. His fragrance has spread through the desert and every grain of sand was touched by his soulfulness. I came to this court in quest of wealth, but as soon as I entered the portico I became the seat of honor, and now I move around this court freed of any desire, like the revolving spheres of heaven." Everything in existence moves in order to gain some benefit except the bodies and souls of God's lovers.

He presented the jug of water and said,

"Take this gift to the Sultan, It is sweet water in a new green jug." The officials smiled, but accepted it as if it were as precious as life itself, because these courtiers had become imbued with the graciousness of the Sultan himself. Regard the Sultan as a reservoir with pipes running in every direction, every one of which gives water sweet to taste. But if the water in the reservoir is brackish and dirty, every pipe will produce the same.

Consider how the grace of that dimensionless Spirit has produced effects on the whole body, and how Intelligence brings the whole body into discipline, and how love, restless and uncontrolled, throws the whole body into madness. For whatever knowledge a master is renowned, you will get the same from his pupils. Theologians, lawyers, grammarians all produce students imbued with their knowledge, and again the master absorbed in the way of Sufism will produce students absorbed in God. And of all these different kinds of knowledge, the best equipment and provision on the day of death is the knowledge of spiritual poverty.

When the Caliph saw the gift and heard the story of the Bedouin, he filled the jug with gold and added other presents, and told his courtiers to help him return by way of the Tigris river: "Since he has come here through the desert, it will be shorter for him to return by way of the river."

When the Arab embarked on the boat and saw the Tigris for the first time, he prostrated himself in humility and thankfulness. "The Caliph is so generous, and how wonderful that he took my gift of water."

Everything in the universe is a jug filled to the brim with wisdom and beauty. This whole universe is a drop of the Tigris of His beauty. His beauty was a hidden treasure, which burst forth and made this earth more resplendent than the heavens. And if the Arab had seen just a branch of the Tigris, he would have destroyed the jug. But the jug is only improved by being shattered: every piece of it dances in ecstasy, though to the limited mind this sounds absurd.

Kabir Helminski
MATHNAWI I, 1252FF